"Nate Larkin turns a biblical and cultural landmine into a divine landmark."

— LEONARD SWEET,
futurist and author of *SoulTsunami*

"The kind of gospel that provokes Nate Larkin to dig into the faith and risk everything is the gospel that gives freedom to the oppressed, and gives men like me the ability to come out of the darkness of isolation and into the experience of genuine community."

— DAN HASELTINE,
lyricist and lead singer, Jars of Clay

"Most men I know urgently need Nate's wisdom and honesty."

— MARK BUCHANAN,
author of *Your God is Too Safe*

"Christian men who love Jesus, but struggle privately with everything that most men struggle with, are about to find a new best friend. Nate Larkin has written the honest, no-holds-barred book they've been waiting for."

— CHARLIE PEACOCK,
music producer

r of *New Way to Be Human*

"Wow! If you are   book. But if you're tired of shallow, clich      iched, this book could change your life!   and, without compro- mise, disarmingly   l thank me for recom- mending it to you

— STEPHEN BROWN,
professor at Reformed Theological
Seminary in Orlando, Florida,
and author and teacher
on the nationally syndicated radio
program *Key Life*.

"Nate Larkin is a man who, along with current-and-future Pirate Monks, is about to change how male spirituality is done. A path toward male soulwork is here—for those with the courage and faith to enter brotherhood and commu- nity. Meet a second Samson, now with vision, brothers, and far less hair."

— PAUL COUGHLIN,
author of *No More Christian Nice Guy*

"You might say that Samson was given the opportunity to see by having both his eyes gouged out. In his wake he left a pile of shattered and broken stones from the temple of Dagon. This motley band of brothers who bear his name, led by the motliest of them all, Nate Larkin, is growing every day in the understanding of their own blind brokenness. And now, another Temple is coming together from the ashes."

— MICHAEL CARD,
songwriter, author,
and host of In the Studio
with Michael Card

"The gospel is said to be a scandal, but it often seems more like a utility: plastic, molded to shape whatever the current need may be. Larkin takes us back and further into the transformative scandal of a gospel that has the power to shape us into the wild lovers of God we were created to be. I read with both terror and wonder, hope and joy. This is a wild book that will introduce you more deeply to the wiles of God, his pursuit of our heart, and the glory of being won by a God so scandalous."

— DAN B. ALLENDER, PH.D.,
President, Mars Hill Graduate School,
and author of The Wounded Heart,
To be Told, and Leading with a Limp

"Nate Larkin's Samson and the Pirate Monks is the most moving book I've read in years! Where can I sign up? I want an eye patch and a parrot. Dallas Willard has said that he does not trust any effort in Christian formation unless it resembles the AA movement in structure and approach. In Samson and the Pirate Monks, Nate grabs your attention with shocking honesty and then describes how he and a band of courageous friends have combined the best of the recovery movement and spiritual formation. This book will change the way we do church."

— GARY W. MOON, PHD,
Vice President and Chair of Integration,
Psychological Studies Institute, and
author of Falling for God and Spiritual
Direction and the Care of Souls

"We don't need another Christian book giving formulas and scripture verses on living the committed Christian life. What we need is a book so openly raw and transparent that we can finally see pieces of our own hidden and shameful selves between the pages. Thanks, Nate, for this courageous, unflinching, dangerous, and most of all honest book that just may help waken the church to what many Christians are actually struggling with without knowing where to turn . . . until now."

— BRAD STINE,
social commentator, comedian,
and author of *Being a Christian Without Being an Idiot*

"Finally someone steps up to address the real truths that have kept men from coming to church."

— BRYAN DUNCAN,
singer, songwriter, author,
and host of *Radio Rehab*.

"Nate Larkin has written a stunningly candid confession of his struggles with sin, and in the process has invited men to face honestly their own struggles. And he has taken it to the next step: outlining a helping and healing process so men wrestling with addictive behaviors can really find hope for change, freedom from moral pollution, and authentic friendships in Christ. This is a great book with an awesome message."

— JACK HABERER,
Editor in chief
of *The Presbyterian Outlook*

"Long before he sat down to commit his thoughts to the page, I watched Nate write about Samson and Pirate Monks with his brokenness, his tears, and his thirst for the mercy and grace of God. And now I have the joy of seeing the fruit of his journey and labor of love when I look into the eyes of men in our church who are a part of the Samson Society—men who are discovering the wonder of the gospel, the necessity of brotherhood, and the hope of change. As his pastor and friend, I'm glad this book is finally in print and not just a part of the gospel tapestry of our local community!"

— SCOTTY SMITH,
Founding Pastor of Christ Community
Church , Franklin, TN,
and author of *The Reign of Grace*

Samson
and the
Pirate Monks

Calling Men to Authentic Brotherhood

by Nate Larkin

Published by
THOMAS NELSON
Since 1798

www.thomasnelson.com

Published in Nashville, Tennessee by Thomas Nelson, Inc.

Thomas Nelson titles may be purchased in bulk for educational, business, fundraising, or sales promotional use. For information, please email SpecialMarkets@ThomasNelson.com.

All Scripture quotations, unless otherwise indicated, are taken from the Holman Christian Standard Bible (HCBS). Copyright © 1999, 2000, 2002, 2003 by Holman Bible Publishers, Nashville, Tennessee. All rights reserved.

Other Scripture references are from the following sources:

The King James Version of the Bible (KJV).

The New King James Version (NKJV), copyright © 1979, 1980, 1982. Thomas Nelson, Inc., Publishers.

The Message (MSG), copyright © 1993. Used by permission of NavPress Publishing Group.

Editorial Staff: Greg Daniel, acquisitions editor; Thom Chittom, managing editor
Cover Design: Don Bailey
Page Design: Walter Petrie

Interior photograph is courtesy of Walter Petrie

Library of Congress Cataloging-in-Publication Data

Larkin, Nate.
    Samson and the pirate monks : calling men to authentic brotherhood / by Nate Larkin.
      p. cm.
    ISBN-10: 0-8499-1459-0
    ISBN-13: 978-0-8499-1459-1
    1. Christian men—Religious life. 2. Men (Christian theology) 3. Male friendship—Religious aspects—Christianity. 4. Samson (Biblical judge) I. Title.
BV4528.2.L37 2007
248.8'42—dc22   2006033600

Printed in the United States of America

07 08 09 10 11 RRD 5 4 3 2

*To Allie
My Faithful Friend*

Contents

Introduction   xi

Part One   1
Confessions of a Preacher's Kid

One: Right Field, Upper Deck   3
Two: Climb, Climb Up Sunshine Mountain   15
Three: The Addicts Sing   27
Four: Death of a Fantasy   39
Five: The Integrity of a Sinful Man   50

Part Two   59
I, Samson

Six: Who Am I?   61
Seven: Walking Lessons   72

Part Three   85
A New Way of Life

Eight: The Rebirth of the Real Me   87
Nine: Call No Man Father   97

Part Four
The Pirate Monks

111

Ten: The Adventure Begins   113

Eleven: How It Works—A Narrated Tour of the Path   125

Twelve: Our Contract—An Annotated Summary of the Pact   169

Acknowledgments   201

Appendix A: A Suggested Samson Society Meeting Format   205

Appendix B: Suggested Topics for Sharing   209

Notes   211

Introduction

MY NAME IS NATE, BUT YOU CAN CALL ME SAMSON. THAT'S the code name my friends have given me, and for reasons you'll eventually understand, I've given the same symbolic name to each of them. We are the Samson Society.

The men of the Samson Society are my best friends. *Real* men. Real *Christian* men. Real *screwed-up* Christian men. Separately we can act like complete morons, but together—together we are a formidable force for good, an alliance to be reckoned with.

I haven't always had friends. When I was little I had playmates, mostly my brothers and sisters. In school I had classmates. I am a congenial sort of guy, usually pretty well-known around town and fairly well liked. In business and at church I have always had plenty of "hello-friends," but not *real* friends, not the kind you can count on to carry your casket and look after your wife and kids when you die. Whenever anyone offered that kind of friendship, I disappeared.

During most of the last twenty-eight years I had only one real friend—my wife, Allie. As far as I knew, she was the only person who knew my crap and loved me anyway.

Being my only friend was hard on Allie. Sure, she wanted me all to herself sometimes. She liked the feeling of togetherness we experienced when my head was actually at home. But she got tired of being the only one who could confront me when I was wrong, advise me when I was confused, and cheer me up when I was depressed. I piled the weight of all my missing friendships onto her and then got mad when she acted like a girl.

I needed friends—comrades—and now I have them. This is the story of how it happened, presented with random commentary about subjects as diverse as Linux, the Bible, baseball, and the killing of Julius Caesar.

I can promise you one thing: the story isn't boring.

Part One

Confessions of a Preacher's Kid

☠ ONE ☠

Right Field, Upper Deck

I LOVE BASEBALL.

I don't *play* the game very well, you understand. When I tried out for the Harmonsburg Little League team, the coach looked me over and sent me into right field. "Where's right field?" I asked. He pointed. I ran toward the far fence, proudly carrying the new baseball glove my father had given me the week before.

When I turned around, the coach was standing at home plate with a bat, knocking ground balls at the infielders. Suddenly he called, "Right field!" I heard a sharp *crack!* and saw the ball shoot into the sky. It climbed like a rocket, higher and higher, almost intercepting a passing bird, then finally—majestically—slowed, stalled, and began plummeting in my direction.

I watched, fascinated, as the ball bore toward me. *I should catch this,* I thought. *I should raise my glove.* But for some reason my arms would not work. *If I don't catch this ball, it might hit me.* I tried again to raise my glove, but it was no use; I was completely paralyzed. *Yes, the ball is going to hit me. It is definitely going to hit me. This is probably going to hur—* The ball struck me full in the face.

After my nose stopped bleeding and I had found my glasses, the coach suggested that I might want to spend some time playing catch before trying out again for the team.

I never played competitive baseball on a real team, but during my teenage years I followed the New York Yankees from opening day to their final out. I couldn't watch them on television, because my family didn't own a television. But I could listen to the games on my transistor radio, and I could read the box scores and check the standings in the *Watertown Times* every afternoon. During night games on the West Coast when the first pitch wasn't thrown until after our bedtime, I tucked the radio under my pillow and whispered developments to my brothers until they fell asleep.

The Football Seats

In the spring of 1993, when the brand-new Florida Marlins took the field at Joe Robbie Stadium for their very first major league baseball game, I was in the stands with my youngest son, Daniel. He was twelve years old at the time, morphing before my eyes, and I was hoping that baseball might give us a common language, a way to communicate during his teenage years. It did. Daniel soon loved the game as much as I did, and we followed the team together while Daniel and the Marlins suffered through adolescence.

By their fifth season, when the Marlins had become genuine World Series contenders and Daniel had become a young man, we owned a pair of season tickets at the ballpark. Actually, "ballpark" is a charitable term. Joe Robbie Stadium was built for football, not baseball. Our seats, a few rows above the rail on the upper deck, held a commanding view of the 50-yard line. They were great *football* seats. We told ourselves that they were good-enough baseball seats, since they gave us an overview of the entire playing field from high above the action.

We loved it when the Marlins were in town. After leaving our car in a five-dollar parking spot somewhere beside the Florida Turnpike, we'd hike to the stadium, ride a tall escalator to the third level, and stand in line for hot dogs and cokes. Then with both hands full and our tickets in our teeth, we'd make the tightrope walk to our seats. After we'd settled in, I'd prop a transistor radio on the armrest between us.

For the next three hours or so, we'd watch the game unfold on the field far below while listening to the play-by-play on the radio. We didn't bother bringing our baseball mitts because no foul balls ever reached our section. We would talk about the players and speculate about strategy. Sometimes when there was a dispute on the infield, other fans sitting around us who didn't have radios would ask us what was going on. When the game was very slow, our section often would invent diversions to pass the time. We were watching baseball from the football seats, and we were happy.

The Baseball Seats

One morning I received a phone call at work, a call that changed my life forever as a baseball fan. It was an invitation to a birthday party for an acquaintance, a wonderful old man named Harry. Harry's son was the majority owner of the Marlins, and he was planning a small celebration for his dad in his luxury box during an upcoming ball-game. I accepted immediately. A couple of days later, a ticket and a VIP parking pass appeared on my desk.

This time when I arrived at the ballpark, the parking lot attendant spotted the purple VIP pass dangling from the rearview mirror of my decrepit Mazda. He directed me toward a special gate, where a guard smiled and waved me through. I drove right up to the stadium, park-ing a few feet away from a canopy-covered walkway that led to an ele-gant entrance. As I approached the entrance, the doors opened and a blonde usher welcomed me inside. She glanced at my ticket and then guided me through a lush lobby—past paintings and trophy cases—to a brass elevator. A moment later we stepped out into a carpeted cor-ridor populated by white-jacketed waiters pushing linen-covered carts. I could hear the soft clink of glassware. The usher led me to an oak door and opened it, revealing a sight that took my breath away.

There, *right there*, just beyond some sofas and theater seats, lay the infield. It was beautiful beyond words. The red-clay diamond, cut neatly into the manicured grass and buttoned in place with immaculate bases, appeared almost close enough to touch. Enthralled, I took a seat at the front of the box and watched as the groundskeepers misted the base paths and chalked the foul lines. Below me, the expensive seats behind the backstop slowly filled up, and the players took the field for warm-ups. Meanwhile other guests filtered into the box behind me.

When the guest of honor arrived, we all applauded and sang "Happy Birthday." Then the owner directed us to a steaming buffet featuring hot dogs—not the foil-wrapped dogs with the soggy buns that I had been buying on the upper concourse, but steamed deli dogs with fresh rolls and all the fixings. They were fabulous and they were free. I ate three. The drinks were also free. I drank three. I was considering a fourth when the owner of the team sat down beside me.

"Are you enjoying yourself?" he asked.

I bubbled like a ten-year-old. "I've never been this close to a game before," I said. "This is fantastic!"

The owner grinned. "You like to be close? Follow me."

He led me back through the luxury box, out the oak door, down the corridor, and into the brass elevator. When it stopped we were in a dim cavern somewhere beneath the stands. I followed him through a maze of concrete columns and into a tunnel, and when we came out of the tunnel . . . *we were on the field!* We were actually in front of the stands in a little cove protected by Plexiglas. It contained a television camera and a half-dozen folding chairs. The umpire, the catcher, and the batter were just a few feet away. The pitcher hurled a fastball and I ducked. The owner laughed. "Looks a little different down here, doesn't it?" he asked. I nodded, unable to speak, and ducked again as a foul tip banged off the Plexiglas screen. He motioned toward a pair of seats and we sat down.

I wanted to stay in those seats forever. I was watching baseball from the baseball seats for the first time in my life, and *this was a different game*. This was not the leisurely ballet of pitch and catch that I had watched from high above the 50-yard line while listening to the radio. This game was lightning-fast, brutal, and unspeakably sublime. A hundred things were happening around me all at once, and even though I didn't understand them all, I could *feel* them. Behind the rhythmic slap of horsehide on leather I could feel the flashing of signs, the coiling of muscles, the subtle adjustments in angle and stance that rippled toward the outfield. I could hear the chatter of the dugouts and the faraway murmur of the crowd. I could sense the concentration of men who had devoted their lives to this very moment. And then in a quick series of explosions, the crescendo of a play and the echoing call of the ump. This, *this* was baseball.

Men of Integrity

When I think about my life as a Christian, it seems to me that I spent my first forty years in the upper deck, watching the gospel from the football seats. I liked those seats just fine. I was in the stadium. I knew God, loved God, and wore his jersey. I didn't really know the other fans in my section, but I enjoyed their company. When we talked, we talked about God and the game. The gospel was far away, but we could still see it, analyze it, and argue about it. We relied heavily on broadcasts from experts who were closer to the field, and when things got slow we entertained ourselves with diversions of our own invention.

I always enjoyed hearing the gospel, even during those years when I was sitting in the upper deck. Its songs and stories captured my imagination, and its pageantry could move me to tears. I loyally followed my favorite preachers, parroting their phrases and mimicking their signature moves. There were those times, of course, when I yearned to move closer to the field, but I didn't seem to have the right ticket.

As I understood it, only men of integrity could play the real game. I thought that preachers and church leaders were Christians for whom personal sin had become a thing of the past, leaving only *semi-sins* such as speeding or grouchiness to serve as sermon illustrations. I believed that big league Christians devoted their days to prayer and Bible study. They no longer experienced fleshly desires because their flesh had been transfigured long ago. And on those rare occasions when they were subjected to temptation, they always made the right

decision. Occasionally a church leader might be caught in an out-
right sin, but that was a rare exception, and the offender was immediately fired or traded to protect the integrity of the team.

My dream was to play in the big leagues someday, but I wasn't sure
how to get there. Nobody seemed to want to play catch, and I couldn't
get the hang of the game just by watching it, listening to talks about
it, reading about it, and practicing on my own.

My hopes for integrity were dealt a terrible blow by puberty.
The natural awakening of my sexual impulses was not a subject I
could discuss openly with anyone, and its manifestations left me
deeply ashamed. My involuntary and progressively obsessive interest in the female form—the rampaging thoughts and physical
responses produced by the flood of new hormones—caused me
indescribable distress. Sunday after Sunday I resolved to conquer
lust, but the climate of shame and secrecy in my religious environment forced me to battle the beast alone. On those terms the battle
was unwinnable.

I occasionally attempted to communicate with others about what
was really going on, but I always did so carefully, not wanting to ruin
my chances of making the team. When it came to issues of sexuality,
I spoke in code, veiling my questions with vague references to "temptation" or pretending to be bothered by anger.

Meanwhile, my religious persona was gaining quite a reputation
for piety. Saint Nate was the kind of kid religious mothers held up as
an example to their children and a reproof to their husbands. I
moved naturally into leadership positions in Christian youth organizations, where the heightened visibility made it all the more necessary for me to hide my sin until I could find a cure for it.

"It is better to marry than to burn" (1 Cor. 7:9), the college chap-
lain quoted with a wink. It was a verse I knew well, a verse I con-
strued to mean that marriage would solve my lust problem. I found a
fabulous woman, and on the day I graduated from college I married
her, but the problem didn't disappear. If anything, it metastasized.
When that happened, I panicked and blamed my wife.

It was at about this time that I was struck by a novel thought. I had been regarding integrity as a *precondition* for entering the ministry, but what if I were looking at it all wrong? What if integrity is really a *product* of the ministry? Surely I would learn the deeper secrets of the Christian life in seminary. Surely I would stop fooling around with lust when it became my *job* to serve God, when I was being *paid* to pray and preach and study the Bible. The more I thought about it, the more certain I became. I would find integrity in the spotlight!

What I Learned in Seminary

Seminary, however, proved to be the nadir of my spiritual experience. For three years, Allie and I lived off-campus in married housing. Allie seldom visited the school and was never able to attend any classes—she was too busy bearing our children and running a day care in our apartment to pay the bills. I spent my days alone, studying. Most of the classes were huge, taught by brilliant professors who had no idea who I was.

On her single visit to our apartment, the seminary's pastor for married students, a hawkish woman in her fifties, sat on our couch with a teacup balanced on her knees and, after verifying our names, brightly asked, "So, how's your sex life?" Stunned, we both said, "Fine," and the interview was over.

In truth, nothing was fine. We were alone, and we were slowly drowning.

The worst part for me came on a trip that Allie and I took to New York City, an outing sponsored jointly by the seminary and a feminist group called Women Against Pornography. Our guide took us on a walking tour of Times Square. We followed her through porn shops as she declaimed about the exploitation of women by the sex industry. She sent us into a peepshow in one of the shops, tokens in hand, so that we could see the horror for ourselves. I got my first look at hardcore pornography with my wife sitting beside me in one of those tiny blackened booths. The flickering images disgusted us both and we couldn't wait to get outside. But at the same time, somewhere deep inside me I could feel a strange and beckoning fascination, as though a cellar door had been opened. Those images lit a fire in me that would burn uncontrollably for nearly twenty years, a fire that smolders still.

Until the Times Square incident, drugstore magazines, pulp novels, and Hollywood movies had fed my secret sexual fantasies. Overnight, however, my taste shifted to more explicit fare, and I soon found myself venturing alone into the seamy underworld of X-rated theaters and sex shops in search of this powerful new drug.

A shameful cycle quickly developed. It would begin with a feeling of emptiness or dissatisfaction, followed quickly by a craving for relief. As the craving grew, previous pledges to resist it would rapidly evaporate, and before long, consciously or unconsciously, I would start formulating a plan. The plan always required deception—a precautionary cover story to account for the time and money I would need for my fix. Sometimes I concealed the plan so well from my conscious self that I was actually surprised when my car turned, apparently of its own volition, into the parking lot of the theater or shop.

The risk of being seen and the thrill of violating a taboo would trigger a rush of adrenaline as I approached the door. I would feel the first surge of dopamine—the mood-altering chemical cascade in the brain so prized by cocaine addicts and long-distance runners—as I perused the merchandise and made my selection. Inevitably, however, the wave of good feeling would dissipate. The euphoria would pass, leaving me disappointed, awash in self-loathing, cursing myself for my stupidity, and promising never *ever* to do that again. I would step back into my regular life with renewed resolve, but before long my inner emptiness and dissatisfaction would start screaming for relief, and the cycle would begin again.

On one of these forays, I stepped out of a peepshow booth and almost bumped into an assistant professor from the seminary. I immediately turned and fled, praying he hadn't recognized me, but a few days later he accosted me in the theological library. He said it was good to know that I was open-minded, and he wanted me to understand that his wife was fully aware of his activities. It made their marriage more interesting. Did my wife feel the same way? I blanched, suddenly remembering that our wives had met. No, I told him, she most certainly didn't. Well then, he said conspiratorially, we both had a very good reason to keep this matter quiet, didn't we?

The habit continued. I didn't perceive it at the time, but my growing dependency on pornography was steadily deadening my heart, drawing me away from my family and every other healthy love. Before long a fog had descended over my day-to-day life. I was seldom present in the moment anymore, living instead in the shameful memory of my last fix or the guilty anticipation of the next one. I avoided deep relationships with other guys, instinctively regarding them as inferiors or rivals and wary of being discovered. I also kept my distance from women. Most of them appeared to me as bodies, not people, and I preferred the safety of imaginary intimacy to the risks of real relationships.

I even retreated from my wife. Allie, who had made a promise before God to be my faithful friend for life, could feel me drifting away from her emotionally, and she couldn't find an explanation for it. As far as she knew, I was an emotionally healthy and self-motivated Christian guy who was bent upon making his mark on the world. Eventually she concluded that I was losing my interest in her because she was defective. Without actually saying so, I agreed.

Ever the sainted martyr, however, I continued to carry on the outward duties of an attentive husband. Unlike some of the other guys I knew, I helped out around the house when I was home, always making sure that Allie knew about the sacrifices I was making. I was very kind and solicitous toward my wife, but in a condescending sort of way, listening to her problems with professional-grade compassion and patiently explaining the things she was doing wrong. I also went to work every day and earned money, carrying a couple of part-time jobs during the school year, preaching in a little country church on weekends, and painting houses during the summers. I figured Allie was pretty lucky to be married to me.

Even my pursuit of pornography, I told myself, was a noble thing. After all, Allie was busy raising three kids and babysitting six others in our tiny apartment during the days, and she just didn't have the energy to perform as a sex goddess every night. It would be unfair for me to expect that of her. On the other hand, sex was my fundamental male need, more important than food or sleep, as essential to my survival as air and water. I would die without it. Going to a sex shop, then, was like stopping at McDonald's on my way home from work to save Allie the trouble of cooking. There were no dirty dishes afterward. I wasn't having an affair. There were no real women involved. I was being faithful to my wife, and considerate too. She wouldn't understand it, of course, so for her sake I had to keep that part of my solicitude secret.

A Professional Christian

Allie and I were still talking, especially in the evenings while under the influence of alcohol, and we both admitted that we were unhappy. As my final year of seminary drew to a close, we agreed that we were in no condition to accept pastoral responsibility anywhere. We were exhausted and confused. We decided that what we needed was to find a Christian community, a healing place where we could rebuild our marriage and reestablish our spiritual lives. A booming new church in south Florida seemed to fit that description, so we turned down offers of employment elsewhere, packed up our stuff, and moved south. A month later, I accepted a position as the church janitor.

Glossy brochures described our new church as a vibrant community of faith, an oasis of devotion and compassion in the Sunshine State. Allie and I were thrilled to join. We made a few friends, eventually finding our way into the "inner circle" of the church. The pastor even invited me to preach on a few occasions.

One cool winter evening, after a weekend men's retreat where I had heard some guys tell their stories, I sat down with Allie and confessed the truth about my struggle with pornography. She was crushed by the news but accepted it bravely, squeezing my hand and reassuring me that she loved me anyway. I promised to leave it all behind. Telling the truth made me feel a lot better, and for a time the compulsion seemed to disappear. *Confession is the key to freedom*, I concluded. *The secret is out, the dragon is slain, and now I can live with integrity.*

Meanwhile my janitorial position at the church was causing problems, because I was finding some unexpected dirt there. As it turned out, the church was not quite as perfect as I had originally believed. There was, in fact, a considerable gulf between the rhetoric of the church and its reality. Incensed by some of the things I was hearing and convinced that my own motives and aims were now entirely pure, I privately confronted the pastor with a list of allegations and demanded that changes be made. One change was made, and quickly. Within hours I was out of a job. A couple of weeks later Allie received an anonymous phone call warning her that if we didn't leave the state within three days, something terrible would happen to me.

We stayed anyway, and about nine months later we started a new church with the help of others who had left the church in an exodus of staff and leaders. We met in a high school auditorium and in no time had collected a congregation of a hundred souls. In my mind I had become a man of integrity, and I was finally embarking on my life's dream as a pastor.

The life of a pastor was intoxicating and isolating. I was now a professional holy man, the man with the answers, and the expert on all things spiritual. A meeting of the church wasn't official unless I was present, and the ideas of others did not become plans without my blessing. People listened when I spoke. I was marriage counselor, professor, confessor, and leader of the expedition. I was indispensable, and I was *very* impressed with myself.

As king of the mountain, I convened the church councils and set the agendas. The pulpit, which was exclusively mine, gave me power to direct the attention of the congregation, define the important issues, and deflect criticism. My authority was absolute, but it was based on the perception that I was the guy in the church who really had his act together. I was the "man of integrity," and it was essential for everyone's sake that I protect that perception at all costs.

So there was no one I could talk to when my marriage and my personal life started to fray under the inevitable pressures of the ministry. When I started going back into sex shops again, there was no one I could tell except Allie, and I couldn't bear to break her heart a second time. Before long the old secret war was raging hotter than ever. Obsessed with lust but unable to address it openly, I found myself talking a lot in my sermons about speeding and grouchiness.

One Christmas Eve I hit a new low. It was a cold night, unusual for south Florida. I was on my way to preach at a candlelight service in a chapel downtown when I saw a girl in a thin coat walking along the avenue. I pulled over to give her a ride. She got in, shivering, and thanked me. Within seconds she had propositioned me, offering oral sex for twenty bucks. As it happened, I had a twenty-dollar bill in my wallet that was earmarked for the offering plate. My heart was in my throat. I said yes, and she showed me where to park.

Afterward I was panic-stricken and sick with guilt. At the church my wife's warm smile and my children's hugs felt like knives. The service started. I fumbled through the Scriptures and stumbled through the sermon like a zombie, thinking all the time that I was a miserable fraud who had passed the point of no return. I had gone beyond fantasy into the real thing. I had been unfaithful to my wife, and no matter how guilty I felt about it I would do it again. That much I knew. A nightmare was hurtling in my direction, and there was nothing I could do to stop it. It was going to hit me, and it was going to hurt.

I was right.

☠ two ☠

Climb, Climb
Up Sunshine Mountain

I'M ONE OF THOSE CHRISTIANS WHO GREW UP IN CHURCH.
In fact, as far as I can tell, I was *conceived* in a church. My parents'
first home was a country meetinghouse, an old clapboard chapel that
sat beside a dirt road. It was an abandoned building when my father
first noticed it late on a July afternoon, badly overgrown and coated
with dust from the Fords and Chevys that sailed past it each day. A
farm kid freshly graduated from Bible school, my dad was driving fast
and praying for God's direction. (That has always been his philosophy. "Don't just sit there waiting for God to tell you where to go," he
says. "Get moving! God won't steer a parked car.") When he saw the
church, he slid to a stop, and then backed up.

The front door was locked, but looking through the windows he
could see a few pews, a platform with a rail, a pulpit, and a piano.
Behind the piano was a door. Dad worked his way along the side of
the building to another window and looked into the back room,
which was unfurnished and cluttered with debris. Then he walked
around the property a few times, surveying the building with a prac-
ticed eye. The church hadn't been painted in years, and it needed a
new roof. He could see electrical wiring but no evidence of indoor
plumbing, central heat, or a phone. It was perfect!

Dad arranged to rent the old church, then worked evenings and

Saturdays refurbishing the sanctuary and converting the back room into a studio apartment. I wasn't there, of course. My arrival was still more than a year away, and five more years would pass before I accompanied him to work for the first time, helpfully inserting nails into my nose and fetching the wrong tools. Still, I can imagine the project. Dad usually worked alone and always at a blistering pace, as though he were working against a stopwatch. A self-taught builder and efficiency expert, he could accomplish more in a day than most guys can in a week. By autumn he was finished.

The day after Thanksgiving, Dad moved his new bride into the one-room apartment and put a sign out front announcing that the church was open for services. He worked a factory job to pay the bills, and Mom helped out by taking some nursing shifts in the local hospital. On Sunday mornings and Wednesday nights they held church, she playing the piano and filling the hall with her clear soprano voice, he stalking the platform and preaching. Sometimes nobody else showed up. It was their first pastorate, and it lasted almost two years.

The Tiger Tamer

My dad is a preacher, but not the bookish, tea-sipping type. He doesn't own a library. When I was a boy, he would make his way to the living room early in the morning while it was still dark, switch on the lamp beside his recliner, and sit with his ten-pound leather-bound King James Bible open in his lap, reading and praying. After breakfast he would assemble his children for family devotions. Then he'd load his tools into the car and go to work.

Dad always held at least one day job, except for one brutal winter when he was injured and we almost ran out of food. The churches he served in those days were small blue-collar congregations, never big enough or rich enough to support a married preacher with a growing family. It was pioneering ministry, the kind of work Dad enjoyed. He worked hard and preached hard. He did not take vacations, and he never played. I played, but not with him.

Mom and Dad did keep me well supplied with playmates. I was their first child, but by kindergarten I had two brothers and two sisters. By third grade I had two brothers and *five* sisters. Our family could double the attendance of a typical Sunday school just by showing up.

The Larkin family on parade at church was a sight to behold. Scrubbed and dressed in our Sunday best—I in a shirt and tie, my twin brothers in matching outfits, the girls in homemade dresses—we would file in together, sit together, sing together, listen together, bow our heads and pray together, all under the careful supervision of our parents.

Anyone who stepped out of line experienced my father's discipline, lightning-quick and stinging. Dad did not believe in reasoning with children or giving them second warnings. He trained his kids like Siegfried and Roy used to train their tigers, back before one ate Roy. Dad was always in control, and Mom was his lovely assistant. Their children learned to behave perfectly in public, much to the delight of adults and the chagrin of other children.

Sometimes Dad would call us up to perform during a church service, either singly or in sets. At these opportunities I strutted, because I was *good* at doing church. My specialties were Bible recitation and singing. Under my mother's tutelage I had memorized entire chapters of Scripture that I could reel off in a very impressive fashion. I had also inherited my mother's singing voice and my father's lungs, a powerful combination. When I sang, church ladies swooned.

Church Ladies

While it was true that God had given men—mainly my father—the major speaking roles in church, ladies usually outnumbered men on Sunday mornings. Several of the more devout ladies attended worship faithfully even though their husbands and teenage sons stayed home. The errant males sometimes did make an appearance on Easter or Mother's Day, jumpy as cats, enduring an hour of religion to gain twelve more months of freedom. After the service, while the ladies dawdled and talked, the unchurched men would congregate in the parking lot, furtively smoking and slowly recovering their masculinity.

The preacher was the captain of the sanctuary, but down in the church basement, in the engine room of the ark, it was the ladies who made things happen. They taught Sunday school, organized covered dish suppers, filled missionary barrels, and ran Vacation Bible School. One lady played the rickety downstairs piano while another led the children in energetic singing, repeating the same playlist week after week until the choruses were permanently embedded in our brains, complete with hand motions. To this day I sometimes find myself singing those choruses in the shower.

"Climb, Climb Up Sunshine Mountain"
"Deep and Wide"
"Rolled Away, Rolled Away, Rolled Away"
"If You're Saved and You Know It"
"I May Never March in the Infantry"
"I'm Going to a Mansion . . . on the Happy Day Express"

When song time was over we would go to our classrooms, where the day's lesson would begin with a flannelgraph presentation, if we were lucky. The teacher would press cutout paper figures against the soft background as the story unfolded, rearranging them with each new scene. Here's Johnny, a bad boy who has been listening to worldly music and disobeying his parents. Johnny is filthy, and he is wearing a ragged robe. But here comes Billy, the Christian boy, smiling and carrying a Bible. Billy tells Johnny about Jesus, and the bad boy kneels to pray. Now *heeeere's Jesus*, handing Johnny a brand new robe, sparkling clean.

"Boys and girls, that's what Jesus does for us when we get saved," the teacher said. "He takes away our dirty sins and gives us a pure robe of righteousness to wear. It's a robe he washed himself, with his own blood. And once you have that new robe, *all you have to do is keep it clean.*"

That was my problem. I could not keep my robe clean.

The Impostor

It should have been easy for me to be a good boy. After all, everyone knew my parents were good, and our home was an official sin-free zone. There was no smoking, swearing, drinking, card playing, or dancing in our house, ever—and no dice. We never went to the movies, and we did not own a television. My parents sometimes played the stereo, rocking out to George Beverly Shea, Tennessee Ernie Ford, the Blackwood Brothers, or one of the singing gospel families who occasionally came through town. Our radio was permanently tuned to the local Moody station.

On Sunday afternoons, while other kids in the neighborhood were riding bikes and playing ball, we took a nap, remembering the Sabbath day to keep it holy. There was no lawn mowing or homework on Sunday, but also no running or jumping or ball playing, no associating with our non-Christian friends, and no loud laughter. Especially on Sundays, we turned our eyes upon Jesus.

On Monday mornings we climbed onto the school bus looking like Christians. My brothers and I sported whitewall haircuts and polished shoes; our sisters wore knee-length dresses. We carried our sandwiches in brown paper bags, not Beatles lunch boxes, and we obeyed the bus driver. At school the teachers loved us.

Outwardly I was a model of rectitude—not perfect, of course, but *good*. Certainly good. If an altercation broke out in class, other students would bring up my name during the investigation—"I didn't start it. Just ask Nathan"—and the teacher would accept my version of events without question. I was above suspicion when something was missing.

No one could have imagined how much time I spent planning the perfect crime. *Just how does one get away with murder or embezzle vast sums of money without getting caught? Is it possible to disappear completely and reappear somewhere else under a new name? What would it take to maintain two identities at the same time, a faultless public life and a fun and dangerous private one?* These were the questions that consumed me whenever I wasn't dreaming about becoming the world's greatest evangelist or president of the United States.

In the adventure stories and mystery books that I devoured, the villains were always making careless fundamental errors, dropping hints and strewing clues as though they *wanted* to get caught. When they boasted about their misdeeds to the tied-up hero, I would think, *Shut up, you idiot! Shut up and get out of there before the police arrive!* But the foolish crook would just keep on talking, sealing his fate with an unnecessary confession.

I was not a careless criminal. I wasn't ready to rob banks, but I did mock the law in small ways with an ease that betrayed natural talent. I could slip through the back door of the corner grocery and pluck a few empty pop bottles from the wooden cases stacked inside, then walk through the front door of the store a few moments later to return the bottles, collect the deposit, and purchase a pocketful of penny candy. At school I could rifle through the teacher's desk for loose change while pretending to look for chalk. I lied convincingly and routinely, even when the truth would have served me better, and I seldom overplayed my hand.

But in church, when Dad or my Sunday school teacher talked about sinners, I knew they were talking about me. When the guilt became unbearable, I would get resaved, usually without leaving my pew. I would silently confess my secret sins and promise Jesus that if he would give me just one more spotless robe I would keep this one clean.

Fat chance. Before the cock crowed thrice, I was filthy again.

I Wish We'd All Been Ready

I knew I was playing a very dangerous game, sinning during the last days. It was bad enough that I could be killed at any time by a freak accident, like the teenager we heard about at youth rallies, the one who decided to give his life to Jesus *tomorrow* but then while driving around with his friends, smoking and listening to loud rock 'n' roll, never heard the whistle and was run over by a train. That was bad enough.

Equally terrifying was the imminent prospect of Christ's second coming, an event the preachers always described as glorious, but one I was in no hurry to see. With my luck, the Rapture would happen or Jesus and the angels would show up just when my party here on earth was about to get started, and I would be forced to miss the whole thing. Unless I was sinning at the time, that is. If I were sinning, I would be left behind to face the Tribulation, which would be even worse.

As I saw it, the safest time for me to die or for Christ to return would be the last night of youth camp, right after the campfire service. My chances of evacuation were still pretty good for the next three to five days—until the morning I overslept and missed my quiet time. Then I would start sinning again, recklessly gambling my eternal destiny on the timing of revivals and youth rallies.

One night when I was eight years old, I dreamed witches were chasing me through a forest. One of the witches grabbed me and I woke up, eyes wide and heart thumping. Unable to calm myself, I got out of bed and went to find my mother.

The door to my parents' bedroom was open, but their bed was still neatly made. I figured Mom must be waiting up for Dad, who was working late as usual. So I headed toward the kitchen, where a light burned softly above the stove. I called her name, but no one answered. Confused, I searched the entire house, moving from room to room with a growing sense of dread. My brothers and sisters were all peacefully asleep, but our parents were nowhere to be found. *They were gone.*

I locked all the doors, turned off the lights, and sat in the darkness trying to think. All the evidence pointed to one awful conclusion. Months had passed since youth camp, and I had been eating a lot of ill-gotten candy lately. Like an idiot, I had wasted the last Sunday service by playing Hangman instead of getting my lamp trimmed and ready. Now the Lord had come like a thief in the night, my parents and Sunday school teachers were all gone, and the communists were probably already surrounding the house. They would start torturing us in the morning.

Suddenly there was a knock at the door. For an insane moment I thought that maybe my father had decided to stay behind to take care of us. He would know what to do! But when I asked, "Who's there?" an unfamiliar female voice said that my mother had sent her and that I should unlock the door and let her in. Obviously, the communists were not wasting any time.

The woman continued talking, giving me her name and telling me that she was a friend of the neighbors. The neighbors' newborn baby was sick, and they had called my mother, who was a registered nurse, for help. Mom had gone over right away, with the understanding that someone would come to our house and stay with us until my father got home. The story sounded plausible. Finally I agreed to let the woman in if she could say, "Jesus is Lord." She passed the test and I unlocked the door.

The next morning Dad cooked our breakfast, saying only that Mom was not feeling well. Later that day at school, one of my friends told me that the baby had died.

Expect a Miracle

The baby's death, like every premature death and chronic illness within our believing community, was a deeply troubling occurrence, a rebuke to our faith and a challenge to our understanding of the power and purpose of the gospel. In contrast to the communion meal that came around only once a month, our church prayed for physical healing at every service. We prayed boldly, *claiming* miracles rather than asking for them, avoiding doubt-laden phrases such as "if it be Thy will," because we knew that God is the Great Physician and that it is *always* his will to heal. In our theology, faith was the only variable in prayer for healing. "Believe and receive" was our formula, and we knew that anyone whose faith was strong enough could walk in divine health right up until the day he died.

And miracles did happen. Mostly they happened in other places— the Carnegie Auditorium in Pittsburgh, where Kathryn Kuhlman preached, for example, or the beautiful campus of Oral Roberts University or the teeming African crusades of T. L. Osborne—but occasionally, like a hole in one, a local prayer would bring spectacular results.

When I was four years old, my dad, who had been complaining of stomach pains for months, suddenly lost consciousness one evening during dinner and fell to the floor, blood trickling from his mouth. Mom called for an ambulance and then telephoned several church ladies to organize a prayer meeting. At the hospital, the doctor diagnosed a perforated ulcer and rushed Dad into surgery. As the church prayed, the doctor opened Dad up . . . and found nothing wrong! The non-Christian doctor was mystified, but we all knew exactly what had happened. Dad was released from the hospital a few days later, and his stomach problems never returned.

As the years passed, this miracle loomed large in my religious consciousness. The fact that prayer had prompted divine intervention in my father's life proved God's existence, and it served as a powerful endorsement of everything my father preached. The miracle should have erased all doubt about spiritual realities from my mind. Yet, despite my status as the son of a recipient of a miracle, I did not always believe that God was listening or that he would answer my prayers. I *said* I believed, and I *tried* to believe, but heaven's unresponsiveness proved that my faith was defective.

I was worse than a sinner. I was also a doubter.

Corned Beef and Cabbage

To make matters even worse, I farted in church.

I remember very vividly a midsummer Wednesday night prayer meeting that followed a family dinner of corned beef and cabbage. When the meal began I was aware, of course, that cabbage is a highly volatile vegetable, one that becomes even more unstable when you boil it with corned beef, but I was hungry. When I asked for seconds, I did not yet comprehend that the delicious broth becomes downright incendiary if you place it on a hard pew in a room with great acoustics.

As always, the midweek prayer meeting opened with a few hymns. Dad took requests, and we sang our way through the first and last verses of "In the Garden," "The Old Rugged Cross," and "Sweet Hour of Prayer," with Sister Rogers clunking along on the piano. Not until halfway through testimony time did I become conscious of something stirring deep within me, a powerful and surging urge to . . . *testify*, if you know what I mean.

There was an ancient bathroom in the basement of the church, but it might as well have been on the moon for all the good it did me, because Dad did not allow bathroom breaks for kids during church. Once he got a service off the ground, you were not free to move about the cabin. I closed my eyes and concentrated on containing myself.

I was so completely absorbed in my struggle that it did not even occur to me that there might be other strugglers in the room—until Dad started taking prayer requests. Suddenly, right in the middle of a long and reverent silence, I heard, from the pew behind me, where my sisters were sitting, the distinctive bark of corned beef and cabbage. My siblings heard it too, and we all immediately ducked and clenched to keep from laughing.

You know what happens when you squeeze an inflated balloon? All the pressure immediately shifts to the other end, and sometimes it pops. Suddenly I found myself right in the middle of *The Shootout at the OK Corral*, my brothers and sisters blasting away. By heroic effort I managed to hold my fire, but I could feel myself weakening. I looked up, and my father caught my eye.

Dad apparently interpreted the sincere, pleading expression on my face as spiritual distress, because he called on me. What could I do? Gripping the pew in front of me and rising halfway to my feet, I said in a strangled voice, "I have an *unspoken* request."

I had heard that expression hundreds of time in my life, and it had never been funny before. This time, however, it seemed like the most hilarious thing anyone had ever said. My siblings were weeping, and I did my best to join them. Dad abruptly said, "Let us pray," which was our signal to turn around and kneel. (That's when I understood for the first time why they call it a *pew*.)

As I waited for the end of the service and the inevitable confrontation with my father, I felt myself sinking into a bottomless miasma of shame. What was wrong with me? Right there in church, during the hour of prayer, something scandalous and profane had occurred—and I had *laughed*. Was nothing sacred? *What was wrong with me?*

Dogs and Cats

I wouldn't say my father was exactly a dog lover, but he was definitely a dog *liker*. We usually had a dog around the house while I was growing up (*around* the house, not inside it), and whenever we lost a dog Dad would come home a few days later with another one.

I think Dad liked them because dogs know their place in the universe. Dogs understand that their job is to be man's best friend. They are loyal, affectionate, and—if you train them right—obedient. You can even teach them tricks. Dad was excellent at training dogs. Give him a rope, and in thirty minutes Dad could teach a dog to come. Give him a rope and a station wagon, and he could break a dog of chasing cars.

No dog is perfect, of course. Our all-time favorite dog, a big shaggy fellow named Boaz, turned out to be an alcoholic. A few times each year Boaz would slip down to the town tavern, which was located conveniently next door to the fire hall. None of the volunteer firemen attended our church, but they were all more than willing to buy a beer for the preacher's dog. Boaz would hang around the bar until it closed, then he'd come stumbling home, bombed out of his mind.

Boaz had a drinking problem, but he was truly sorry about it. He'd stand there in the morning with bloodshot eyes, listening patiently as Dad yelled at him and tied him to a tree, and he would repent. A few days later Dad would let him loose again, and for the next few

months Boaz would stay around the house, docile and obedient—
until the next time.

Dad liked dogs, but everyone knew he *hated* cats. My father's
hatred of cats was one of his defining characteristics. I think what he
found most infuriating about felines was their supreme indifference
to authority. Cats do not have masters. They take their own counsel,
and they really don't care what you think. The three most wasted
words in the English language are "Here, kitty kitty."

Cats are unpredictable. Sure, a dog might go off now and then and
get drunk, but afterward he will always come home. A cat, on the
other hand, will just disappear one day without any notice and will
stay away for days, weeks, or even months. No one knows where cats
go. Then one day he'll come strolling back through the door, looking for lunch.

When I was a kid, it seemed to me that God liked me for the same
reasons—and in the same ways—that Dad liked dogs. I was God's pet.
He had brought me home with the expectation that I would be loyal,
obedient, and useful. All God wanted was for me to be a good dog.

I *wanted* to be a good dog, I really did. There was always a part of me
that sincerely loved God. But there was *another* part of me, a *cat* part.
The cat in me was defiant and wild and unpredictable, and it didn't
care about God in the least. When it sinned, it sinned with impunity.

At every revival, youth rally, and campfire service, I laid that cat
on the altar and did my best to kill it. Still, as everybody knows, cats
have multiple lives. Sometimes the cat would go away for a while,
but eventually, after the music had died away and all the Christians
had gone home, he would come strolling back in, looking for lunch.

I desperately wanted the dog to be the *real me*, but my inability to
behave like a good dog for very long led me to suspect, in moments
of despair, that I was really a cat.

⚐ three ⚐

The Addicts Sing

DURING MY BOYHOOD, I WAS BLISSFULLY UNAWARE OF MY family's long and painful experience with addiction. Sure, I heard a few things about my father's wild teenage years, the rebellious period that ended when he got saved and dropped out of high school to attend Bible college, but I had no idea that *his* father, my kindly and devoted Grandpa Larkin, had spent twenty years as a bitter backslider, irresponsible and unfaithful, while Dad was growing up. I also had no idea that my *mother's* father, a full-time steelworker and part-time farmer, had terrorized his family with towering rages. To me he was jolly Grandpa Hill, a lover of purty scenery and waterpunkins. Not until years later, after he retired and my grandmother finally left him at the urging of her children, did I learn of Grandpa's violence and his philandering ways.

By then I was surprised by the information, but not by the revelation that my family had been hiding it from me. We were Christians after all, living in pre-Watergate America, before "cover-up" became a crime and "codependent" became a word. We did not hang our dirty laundry in public, nor did we advertise the fact that our laundry ever got dirty. Our family's code of silence was intended to protect the family name. It also protected the name of Jesus, with whom we were publicly identified. As I understood it, we needed to maintain a "good witness" before the watching world, even if we sometimes had to lie a little to do it.

In a way I envied non-Christians because they were not saddled with the daily responsibility of keeping up appearances. One of my favorite people in the world was Uncle Junior, who lived in a nice trailer with my aunt Sadie and went fishing on Sundays instead of going to church. Uncle Junior was loud, and he always said exactly what was on his mind. He swore a lot. He drank Genesee beer and smoked Lucky Strikes and subscribed to *Playboy* magazine, and he was very kind to me.

Uncle Junior and Aunt Sadie had two daughters but no sons. On two consecutive summers they invited me along on their annual vacation, a weeklong stay in a fishing cottage on Black Lake. Every afternoon Uncle Junior and I would go down to the dock and climb into his aluminum fishing boat. He would fire up the Evinrude and we'd go bouncing across the lake to the package store, where I would stay with the boat while he went inside to buy packages. When he returned, Uncle Junior would hand me a quart bottle of ginger ale wrapped in a brown paper bag. He'd have one too.

Those summers gave me my first taste of the Vegas Effect, the feeling that the normal rules of behavior no longer apply when you're away from home. At Black Lake, I played crazy eights with my cousin Marsha, read comic books, said "crap," and listened to rock 'n' roll on the radio. It was quite a relief when youth camp finally rolled around later in the summer and I could get resaved.

I still think about Uncle Junior sometimes. When I was sixteen, he killed himself with a shotgun. I don't know why.

The City on a Hill

We moved around a lot while I was growing up. On three separate occasions we moved to the Pentecostal Bible college where Dad had studied for the ministry. We moved there for the first time before my second birthday, when Dad agreed to run the school's dairy farm. We returned twice during my elementary and junior high years so he could serve as head of maintenance and construction.

In some ways these positions suited Dad well. He loves farming, and he can fix or build almost anything. But Dad is a pioneer at heart, a preacher with a strong independent streak, and he chafes under the bureaucratic constraints of bosses and budgets and boards. After two or three years at the Bible college, Dad would receive a call to a new church and we would move again.

Looking back, I consider my days at the Bible college the best of my childhood. It was a beautiful place to grow up. Originally a Wesleyan Methodist seminary, the old campus sat on a hill overlooking a town. Sloping lawns and magnificent trees surrounded its rambling brick buildings, their columns and balustrades gleaming white. Behind the school was a dairy, the barn barely two hundred yards from the cafeteria, so that when the wind was right you could drink your milk and smell where it came from all at the same time.

In a weird way, living at the Bible college was like growing up in Vatican City. The school was the spiritual center of our nondenominational denomination. Missionaries from around the planet climbed its granite steps, and celebrity preachers made personal appearances in its chapel. When I was little, it seemed to me that the only Christians in the world either attended our school or were connected to it in some way. Later I learned that there are indeed other Christians in God's army—but we were the *Marines*. And I was proud to serve.

As a campus kid, I belonged to a special family. The male students, dressed like cadets in their navy blazers and gray trousers, saluted me in the hallways. Laughing groups of female students, gorgeous in their long, pleated plaid skirts and collared white blouses, their long hair piled high and sprayed solid as waterpots, swept past me on their way from class like Bible women returning from a well, and greeted me by name.

My friends and I rode our bikes on the college sidewalks, wrestled on the lawns, climbed high in the trees, ran on the porches, and played dodge ball in the old gymnasium. We took our meals in the college cafeteria, went to church in the college chapel, and met for Sunday school in college classrooms. We even went to school on campus, since—in an arrangement unthinkable today—the local school district operated a public elementary school on the first floor of a religious classroom building *while the Bible was being taught upstairs*.

I can clearly remember struggling at my desk with a Social Studies test in the third grade. As I closed my eyes and asked God for the answers, I heard through the open windows the voices of a hundred Bible college students—my brothers and sisters in Christ—singing and interceding on my behalf. I was not alone. I smiled, and the answers came.

Scribes and Philistines

Not long after reading *The Cross and the Switchblade* (Spire, 1965), I met my first addicts. I could tell they were addicts because they arrived at the Bible college in a van with "The Addicts" painted on the side. They were a group of ex-gang members from Spanish Harlem who now toured the country singing and testifying for Jesus.

The leader of the Addicts was a Puerto Rican guy named John Gimenez. John was like Nicky Cruz, only tougher, and he was a great promoter. His group already had an album out on the Word label, titled *The Addicts Sing*, and John was talking about a movie deal. (The movie, starring John Gimenez, did come out eventually, but it was overshadowed by the cinematic version of *The Cross and the Switchblade*, which featured Pat Boone as David Wilkerson and Eric Estrada as Nicky Cruz.) John had recently received God's call to the ministry and had promptly enrolled in Bible college. Naturally, he brought his posse with him.

One of the great things about our college was that we did not get all hung up on formalities like proficiency exams or high school transcripts or, for that matter, high school diplomas. If you were called by God to preach, we would find a place for you. You might say that we had the same entrance requirements for preachers that the University of Miami has for football players.

Riding my bike, I followed the van until it parked outside the cafeteria. The addicts got out and looked around, all cool in their slicked hair and pointed shoes. Then a cow mooed, and one of them jumped back into the van. That addict, I learned later, was Snuffy, a former glue sniffer with a battered face. Years of active addiction had destroyed Snuffy's nasal membranes, making it impossible for him to pronounce certain consonants. He was a sweet guy who introduced himself as Hnuffy and made no secret of the fact that he loved Jehuh.

Once they'd grown accustomed to the place, the addicts plunged right into community life at the Bible college. One Sunday morning I arrived at the boys' Sunday school class to find that we had a substitute teacher—John Gimenez! John flipped through our Sunday school quarterly, winced, and tossed it aside. Then he sat down and told us his testimony. It was an exciting story, full of rumbles and zip guns, "Mary Jane" and heroin. John rolled up his sleeve, flashed his jailhouse tattoos, and showed us how he used to shoot up. He told us how lucky we were to know Jesus at such an early age.

The next Sunday, after looking around the chapel during the morning service and noticing that our regular teacher was still absent, I raced to my classroom for the Sunday school hour, hoping to find John Gimenez again. He wasn't there, but another one of the addicts was filling in. I don't remember this guy's name—I think he dropped out after just a few weeks—but I do remember that he told us a Bible story I had never heard before. The story went something like this:

Jesus was da leader of a group called da "Disciples." (Dey wasn't a *gang*, 'cuz dey was all Christians. Dey was just a group.) Now dere *was* two gangs in da city—da Scribes and da Philistines. Da Scribes and da Philistines hated each udder, but dey hated da Disciples more, an' dey was always out ta get 'em.

Anyway, dere was dis Philistine chick named Mary. She wanted ta quit da Philistines an' join da Disciples, but da Philistines wouldn't let her. So one day, Mary *sneaks away* from da Philistines' turf, and she's on her way to da Disciples' turf, but da Philistines *see* her, an' dey *chase* her, an' dey *catch up* wid her in a vacant lot, and dey start to *throw stones* at her. *Big* stones.

Just den, Jesus and da Disciples pull up. Now da littlest Disciple, David, he has dis *slingshot* dat shoots *real little stones*, like about a .22. David runs up and shoots da leader of the Philistines right in da head and kills 'im.

An dat's how Mary became a Disciple—

Not long ago I bought a copy of the album *The Addicts Sing* from a collector. It cost me forty bucks, but it was worth it to hear those guys sing again. I noticed that on the front and back of the album, the record company had printed very prominently "Nine Former Addicts." *Former* addicts. That would have been a vital distinction in our world, where it was impossible for a Christian to be an addict. To us, an addict was a drug user who needed to get saved. Once he got saved, he was not an addict anymore. Our key verse was also printed right there on the front of the album: "Therefore if any man be in Christ, he is a new creature: old things are passed away; behold, all things are become new" (2 Cor. 5:17 KJV).

You know that section in Romans 7 where the apostle Paul wrote about not doing what he wants to do and continuing to do what he hates? That, the preachers told us, is supposed to be understood *in the past tense*. Paul was describing his sinful life *before he got saved*.

Fortunately, I had been saved early, so I didn't have to worry about ever becoming addicted to anything.

Dreams and Destiny

The church ladies predicted I would be a preacher when I grew up, a preacher just like my dad, and I knew they were right. After all, anyone serious about becoming a gold medal Christian naturally aimed for the ministry. (Unless that person was a girl, of course. In that case, her best option was to take piano lessons so she could *marry* a minister.) Granted, I might earn silver or bronze by entering some other form of "full-time Christian service," becoming a missionary or a gospel musician for example, but second-tier respectability would mock my heritage. I had been born into the priestly class, and preaching was my destiny.

A couple of times when we were alone, my mother carefully suggested that I might think about becoming a doctor. A Christian doctor. Maybe a missionary doctor. I could sense that the subject was important to her, so I listened. Mom had left medical work before I was born, but she spoke with great conviction about the joys and challenges of caring for the sick and injured. Doctors, she said, are heroes. Doctors make a difference.

She grew animated when I asked her about medical training. The Catholic teaching hospital where she had studied was a wonderful place, full of compassion and hope. She said that the only part of the hospital she didn't like was the top floor. That was the mental ward, a dismal domain with steel doors and padded rooms, and she hated being assigned to work there.

In order to spend quality time with us, Mom eventually started a program for her five oldest children, something she called "Nights Up." In our house, kids' bedtime on school nights was eight o'clock, but if it was your Night Up (my night was Monday) you got to stay up, just you and Mom, *until eight thirty!* Some of my warmest childhood memories are of Monday nights with Mom. While the other kids were in bed and Dad was at work, Mom and I would pick a subject at random from the encyclopedia, and I would read the article aloud while she ironed. Some nights, when we couldn't think of a subject, I would read a selection from the *Boys Life Treasury of Adventure Stories* instead. Mom always complimented my reading. She said if I wanted to, I could be on the radio someday.

One afternoon in mid-June, days before the start of summer vacation, I returned from school just in time to see an ambulance pulling away from the back door of our apartment building. I ran to my parents' room, where a neighbor lady was tidying up. The lady patted my head and explained that the doctors had decided to send Mom to the hospital for a short rest. Everything was going to be okay.

During the next year, I would see my mother twice.

Harmonsburg

My mother—the beautiful, funny, brilliant person at the center of my world—had suffered a severe schizophrenic breakdown. She was mentally ill, a condition deemed too disturbing and confusing for young minds like mine. As the days and weeks went by, I pressed my father and the neighbors for details about her condition but received only vague information. Mom was tired and she wasn't feeling well. Doctors were helping her. Eventually I learned that she had been transferred to the hospital in her hometown, where people who knew and loved her were caring for her. Mom was now a patient in the hospital where she had received her nursing training.

Dad was obviously unable to provide and care for eight children by himself. He sent my three little sisters (the youngest only six months old) to live with relatives who had agreed to serve as foster parents until Mom got better. When school ended, he dispersed us five older kids to the homes of other friends and relatives. I traveled light, keeping my clothes in a paper bag. Every few weeks Dad would show up where I was staying and drive me somewhere else.

For two sweltering weeks in July, I lived with a farm family I barely knew. The farmer was a former alcoholic who had been saved under my father's ministry. He and his wife, an imposing woman who watched soap operas in the kitchen during the afternoons, had a son my age. They also had a beautiful teenage daughter who enjoyed sunbathing in the backyard.

I would have liked to stay around the yard during the day, but the boy and I were sent into the front pasture between milkings to keep the cows out of the road. The county highway department had torn down the farmer's fence during a road-widening project, and the farmer was furious about it. As we baked under the sun and threw dirt-clods at the cows, the boy eventually confessed to me that his father had backslidden and was drinking again. It really bothered him that his father was going to hell.

Over the summer, Dad resigned his position at the Bible college and took a construction job in Pennsylvania, about an hour from the hospital where Mom was being treated. He rented an old house in the country, and when school started again in the fall, he brought us five older kids there to live with him. Aunt Sally, one of my mother's younger sisters, came to live with us too. Though barely out of her teens, Aunt Sally was bubbly and warm and maternal. She created a family atmosphere in that old house, and despite my mother's absence I actually had a pretty good year.

I made two friends in Pennsylvania. The first was Janey, a red-headed tomboy who lived next door. Janey was a year younger than I was, but we shared an interest in cowboys and Indians. On my birthday she chased me, caught me, pinned me, and *kissed* me right on the face. I *hated* it.

And yet . . . I didn't.

My other friend was Larry, who sat behind me in the fourth grade. Larry and I were natural allies, since we were both geeks. I liked to read the encyclopedia; he played the accordion. We had other things in common too. For example, my father was a preacher and Larry's father owned the local tavern. One day after school Larry took me into the tavern to meet his dad. The building was unimpressive from the outside, a swaybacked structure with curled shingles and peeling paint, but inside I found a sanctuary, cool and dark. The congregation was gathered along the bar, where Larry's dad officiated with a solemnity I instantly recognized.

One Sunday after church, Dad drove us to the hospital to visit Mom. This was my first chance to see her since she had been taken away, and I had been looking forward to it ever since Dad had announced that she was finally ready for visitors. I made a card for her the night before, an ornately crayoned get-well card with a travel theme, and during Sunday school I privately rehearsed a dozen versions of our reunion.

At the hospital, a nun walked with us to an elevator, where she pressed the button for the top floor. *The top floor.* Suddenly I understood.

The nun directed us to a visitors' lounge, where we sat beneath a crucifix and waited. A buzzer sounded. A lock clicked. A door opened, and the nun came into the waiting room leading a shuffling patient wearing a gown and robe. *This woman was not my mother.* Dazed and disoriented, she looked at me with uncomprehending eyes and then looked away.

"Your children wanted to see you," Aunt Sally said. "Aren't they getting big?"

I handed my get-well card to the woman who was my mother. She said thank you, but didn't open it. We didn't stay long.

Months passed. Finally, on Mother's Day weekend, the hospital released Mom for a three-day visit with her family. We kids were waiting anxiously by the window when the car pulled up. The doors opened and my grandmother stepped out, followed by a woman who *looked* like Mom. We ran to the door. It *was* Mom, but within seconds I sensed that something was still terribly wrong. This was my mother, but her hugs felt artificial, her laughter forced.

As the visit unfolded, Mom said and did bizarre things. She scared me, and I spent most of the weekend outside, playing with Janey.

On Sunday night I was on my way to bed, slipping past my father's bedroom, when I heard Mom call my name. I stopped and looked inside the room. She was lying in bed, her hands folded on the covers, her hair glossy on the pillow. She called my name again, and as I walked toward the bed I could see that *it was really her! It was my mom!* I ran to her. She hugged me, held me, whispered in my ear. She told me that she loved me and was very, very proud of me. Then, before sending me off to bed, she said she hoped I would never become an orphan.

Next afternoon at school, I was so engrossed in the encyclopedia that I didn't hear the teacher call my name. Larry poked me. I looked up and saw my father standing in the doorway. "Get your things together, Nathan," the teacher said. "You're going home early today."

When I reached the hall I found my sisters there, standing hand-in-hand with a family friend, a Bible student named Al. We walked out the front door of the school and got into the car, kids in the backseat. Dad started the engine. Then he turned it off again, put his head on the steering wheel, and started to cry. Al turned around and told us that our mother had died.

My sisters started whimpering. I tried to cry, but couldn't. All I could say was "How?"

Al looked helplessly at Dad. Dad said, "She just got sick and died. She didn't suffer."

When I was sixteen years old, Dad finally told me that Mom had committed suicide. She had disappeared quietly that morning after we left for school, and Aunt Sally had found her hanging from the plumbing in the basement.

When I was forty years old, my stepmother gave me a letter that Mom had written to me before she died. Mom had left two letters, one for my father and one for me. In an elegant flowing hand, she wrote that she was sorry she was sick. She knew it wasn't fair to me or my brothers and sisters, or to Dad, or to Aunt Sally. She wanted to get well, she really did, but she knew she didn't have the faith to get healed.

We buried her in Harmonsburg, Pennsylvania, down the street from the elementary school, next door to the Little League field. Then we moved back to the Bible college.

Larry Redux

One night about nine years ago, I was working late in my Ft. Lauderdale office when the telephone rang. When I answered it, a male voice I didn't recognize asked, "Is this Nathan Larkin?"

"Yes," I said. "Who's this?"

"Is this the Nathan Larkin who used to live in Harmonsburg, Pennsylvania?"

My heart lurched at the mention of the long-forgotten town. "Well," I said neutrally, "I spent a year there once, a long time ago. Why? Who *is* this?"

The man crowed. "Nathan! Wow! You *will not believe* how long our family has been looking for you! Can you stay there? *Stay right there!*" And he abruptly hung up.

A few minutes later the telephone rang again. It was a different guy this time. He said, "I don't know whether you remember me or not, but we were friends back in the fourth grade. My name is Larry."

"Larry!" I said. "*Of course* I remember you! How *are* you? *Where* are you? What have you been doing for the last thirty years?"

Larry asked me about my life, and then he told me about his. After high school, Larry had become a professional accordion player. He had made it big on the polka circuit. For years he and his band traveled around the country, playing the big dances, selling records, and living the fast polka life.

Success, however, could not fill the emptiness in Larry's soul. With the help of Al-Anon, a companion program to AA, he began to recognize the legacy of his alcoholic father, his own emotional immaturity, and eventually, his deep spiritual need.

"Nathan," Larry said, "you were the first person who ever told me about Jesus. Do you remember those talks we used to have after school?"

"Yes," I said. (I was lying. I didn't remember a thing.)

"I never forgot them either," Larry said. "So one day I got down on my knees and asked Jesus to take over my life. And that's when everything changed. I quit the road, hung up my career, and applied to college. After college I went to seminary. Now I'm a minister— I'm the pastor of a Methodist church. And I'm still married! God has given me a wonderful wife. We just had our first child, a boy. We named him Nathan."

⚑ four ⚑

Death of a Fantasy

A MEMORY. NOT LONG AFTER ALLIE AND I MOVED TO south Florida, Allie took a job as an aerobics instructor in a women's health club. We didn't own a car at the time, but the club was within walking distance of our apartment. One night after work, Allie rushed into the apartment wide-eyed and breathless, frantically locking the door behind her. She told me that we needed to get a car. She couldn't make that walk anymore. She said some creep had driven past her slowly, staring, and then had circled back to do it again. Allie had forgotten to take a change of clothes to work, so she was still wearing her aerobics outfit and athletic shoes on her way home. After the guy's third pass, she had taken off running, and she hadn't stopped running until she reached our door.

I had never really noticed women on the streets before, but now, following my Christmas Eve encounter with a prostitute, I started seeing them everywhere. It surprised me how many there were. Not every solitary woman was a hooker, of course, but there were plenty of girls on the street who were hoping to jump into a car with a stranger and earn a few bucks. Most of them were probably drug addicts, and there was no telling what diseases they were carrying.

This was insane. Stupid. Incredibly dangerous. More than that, it was wrong, morally reprehensible, a betrayal of my wife, and a blatant violation of ethical standards established by God. I could not believe I was cruising the streets looking for hookers, but I was, and I couldn't stop. There was a thrill to it, the same kind of feeling I had experienced in sex shops, and I found the feeling irresistible.

The actual sexual encounters were squalid, humiliating affairs. After each one I felt so used and rotten that I wanted to die. On my way home, I often screamed at God, banging on the steering wheel and begging him to relieve me of this terrible wickedness, to take the urge away, but the heavens were silent. After a while, I started wondering whether God was listening, whether he cared about me anymore, or whether he even existed at all.

Determined to fix myself, I pored over popular devotional books during my study times—especially books about holiness and victorious living—hoping to find the magic combination of concepts and disciplines that would enable me to reclaim my integrity. I signed up for seminars, sought out visiting preachers, and on a couple of occasions even submitted to prayer for deliverance from demonic oppression. When these measures brought no lasting relief, I expanded my search, venturing into the fields of psychology and self-help. I was hunting desperately for a private solution to my private problem, and like the guy who lost his chewing gum in the henhouse, I thought I found it several times. Nothing, however, worked for very long.

Throughout these turbulent years, my private prayers always began with the plaintive plea "forgive me." I approached God cringing and groveling, knowing that I was a horrendous disappointment to him and wondering how much longer he would put up with me. I kept pledging to do better, but the resurgence of hope I felt with every fresh start was soon overwhelmed by another failure and a tidal wave of despair. I simply could not achieve integrity.

Finally, after five years in the ministry, I quit. Sex scandals featuring prominent clergymen were all over the national news, and a local Christian politician had just been busted for patronizing a prostitute. I knew I was next. Staying in my current job was tantamount to suicide. If my family and I were going to survive, I would have to get out of the limelight and find another line of work.

Working Late

The lame excuses I gave for quitting the ministry left many people baffled. Our parishioners were gracious about it, but some of them struggled with feelings of abandonment. Dad called several times to tell me about job openings in other churches. He regarded my withdrawal from the ministry as temporary, but I knew that I could never go back. At the age of thirty, with a wife and three kids, I was leaving the only career I knew. What was I going to do?

Amazingly, a guy from the church offered me an office job in his construction consulting company. I learned the business quickly, and a couple of years later two other fellows offered me a partnership in a new engineering firm. I took it. Now reasonably secure in a second career, I set about becoming a responsible Christian layman.

Allie and I had joined a church after leaving the ministry, but reentry into civilian life proved harder than I expected. Sitting in the pew was especially difficult. I found it almost impossible to listen to a sermon without critiquing it on technical grounds. Allie, who was grateful for any new voice in the pulpit, quickly tired of my relentless criticism and asked me to keep my complaints to myself. She said that if I had been present for the Sermon on the Mount I would have said that Jesus should have been better prepared.

I eventually stopped going to preaching services, volunteering to teach Sunday school instead. As the years passed I taught kids of all ages, from kindergarten to high school. I was a popular teacher, probably because I genuinely enjoyed interacting with students. In talking and playing with kids I was revisiting my own childhood and, in a way, trying to remake it. As a bonus, I found that giving myself away for a few hours each week helped me feel a little better about myself.

Allie and I enrolled our kids in a local Christian school, where I was soon elected to the school board. When my term expired, the board offered me a full-time job as the school's executive director, and I foolishly accepted it. I don't know what I was thinking. I'm a terrible administrator and always have been. Popular at first, I eventually

succeeded—through ignorance, impulsiveness, and sheer arrogance—
to alienate a significant percentage of the faculty, staff, and students.

Aware that I was performing poorly and awash in feelings of shame
and self-pity, I retreated into isolation while making valiant efforts to
change. It was no use. I was floundering, and to make matters worse,
I was returning to my favorite mood-altering drug with ever-greater
frequency. Our home life was in shambles. Allie was miserable, and I
was afraid. After two years at the helm of the Christian school, I
resigned and went back to the quiet anonymity of engineering.

Eventually I reconciled myself to the ugly truth. I was a failure as
a minister and a leader. I was a huge disappointment to everyone,
especially God and Allie, and the best I could hope for was to live
out the rest of my days in a moral and spiritual twilight. There was
no hope for change.

By now I had stopped picking up street hookers because my
improved income made it possible for me to visit strip clubs and mas-
sage parlors instead. My job occasionally took me out of town, and I
sometimes hired call girls when I was on the road. To make matters
worse, I now had a highly efficient new source for my drug. A mar-
velous medium, the Internet, was capable of delivering prodigious
amounts of pornography directly to my desktop, where I could con-
sume it in the privacy and safety of my office. I started "working late"
several times a week, eventually logging thousands of hours on the
World Wide Web downloading porn.

While I was "working," my kids were growing up. Allie was virtually a single mom now. Sure, I occasionally showed up to act like
Super Dad, dramatically driving the family to the beach or whisking
them away for a surprise weekend trip to Disney World. I bought
things for Allie. I took my youngest son to baseball games, and at
Allie's insistence I had a weekly date with my teenage daughter, but
on a day-to-day basis I was mostly absent from my family. Allie was
alone, emotionally isolated, abandoned by her best friend. She is
certainly no fool. On some level Allie knew what was going on, but
she elected not to push it, not to ask too many questions. She was

holding her breath for the sake of the kids, and she was praying like crazy for a miracle.

My business partners didn't say anything to me either, although they certainly must have noticed my declining productivity. I had lost the ability to concentrate for any length of time. I regularly disappeared from the office during the day, making up for my absences by "working late" after everyone was gone. My creative output was pitiful.

One of our employees, a systems administrator and writer named Dan, did make a courageous effort to throw me a lifeline. One morning after a long night of "working late," I found a sealed envelope on my keyboard. Inside was a note from Dan, suggesting that based on my computer activity I might be addicted to pornography and that I should get some help. He gave me a name and a phone number, but I didn't bother to call because I no longer believed that help was possible. What's more, I had adjusted. He was probably right—I probably was an addict—but I had finally settled into a state of miserable equilibrium. Life sucked, but I had grown accustomed to it. The highs weren't very high anymore, and the lows weren't very low. I had gone numb, and like a man in the final stages of freezing to death, I really didn't mind.

The Miracle Begins

We moved from south Florida to Tennessee at the invitation of our oldest son and his wife. It happened very quickly. One Friday evening our daughter-in-law, Samantha, called to tell us that we would soon be grandparents, and she asked whether we would consider moving to Tennessee to be near our grandchild. I was working in Tampa at the time, staying in a hotel between two strip clubs and getting very little work done. Allie called me with the news, and I caught the next plane to Nashville. With Samantha's assistance, two days later I found an old bungalow on a quiet street in the historic town of Franklin. On my way back to the airport I arranged for Allie to come and see the house.

Aboard the plane, I found myself seated beside a smiling older woman who clearly wanted to talk. *Great.* We exchanged pleasantries. She was a realtor from Tampa, returning from a week in Franklin, where she had been visiting her grandchildren. Did I have any grandchildren? *Not yet, but we're expecting our first in about eight months.* Was I from Nashville? *No, but I had just spent my weekend in Franklin, looking for a house.* Did I, by any chance, know anything about Christian music? *Yes, a little.* Well, perhaps I'd heard of her son-in-law, Steve Green? *Of course. Great voice.* So was I a Christian, then? *Yes.* In that case, she said, when I moved to Franklin I absolutely *must* visit Christ Community Church, where Scotty Smith preached, and I must drop in on George Grant's Sunday school class. I told her I would. She made me promise. I promised, and went to sleep.

I didn't realize it at the time, but my world had just turned. Barely four months later I would be listening to the gospel in a church where it was safe to admit brokenness, where the pastor talked about his own sin in the present tense and celebrated the mercy of God every Sunday. Here I would hear about the covenant of grace and the steadfast love of our heavenly Father. I would be reminded week after week that I am an adopted son of God, no longer an orphan, and that my Father never disowns his own. Finally—and this was the greatest miracle—it was in this church where I would meet many of my future comrades, the men whose friendship God would use to radically rearrange my life.

I did not approach these men willingly, however. I only reached out for help in a last-ditch effort to save my marriage.

Our first few weeks in Franklin were idyllic. Away from my familiar Florida haunts, I swore off pornography and illicit sex and found that my interest in Allie was rekindled. My wife responded ardently. We sat together in church and Sunday school and talked about the messages afterward. We laughed, went for walks, and worked together in the yard.

Eventually, however, I found a job in Nashville, a town where at that time dozens of sex-oriented businesses were openly flourishing. I also set up my computer in the house and hooked up to the Internet.

My new job did not pay well. We started running low on money. Pressures mounted, and before long I was back to my old tricks, lying to Allie and using lust to medicate my fear.

One night Allie caught me looking at pornography on my computer. She cried. A few days later she found a condom I had inadvertently dropped in the bathroom. This time she didn't cry. Instead, she sat down beside me in the bedroom, showed me the condom, and said, calmly, that she would not allow herself to be hurt anymore. She cared about me as a person, but she no longer trusted me, did not respect me, and to be honest, didn't like me very much. From now on, we would live separate lives.

We could stay married—she wasn't leaving—but she would be finding her own friends and making her own decisions. I was on my own. She hoped I would find help, but she doubted I had the humility to accept help from anyone. She was sorry I had decided to walk away from her. She thought my decision was a crazy one, but she wasn't going to fight it anymore.

That was it. Allie had given me the gift of desperation. The very next day I started looking for someone to talk to. This time I was ready, really ready. And this time, by God's grace, I found the right guy.

Stepping Out

For a number of reasons, I did not call a professional counselor. The biggest reason: I was broke. Thanks to years of addiction and a long series of bad financial decisions, Allie and I were now scraping for grocery money. Also, I had always enjoyed counseling, but it hadn't done me much good. Counseling sessions usually turned into mental tennis matches for me. I enjoyed matching wits with an opponent, maneuvering him carefully to one side of the court, concealing critical information until the last minute, and then blasting a crosscourt return that left him looking flat-footed and stupid. I lied to counselors—a dumb thing to do when you're paying a person to listen to you—if that's what it took to win. Or sometimes, if I liked the counselor and felt sorry for him, I'd blink and nod and pretend to be enlightened. "Gee, thanks," I'd say. "You really changed my life."

I also decided not to talk to a pastor. Our new church was huge, and I knew it would probably take a year to get an appointment with the top guy. Also, I wasn't eager to advertise my problems in a place where I secretly hoped to become important someday. Better to keep up the respectable facade while I worked things out on the side. Besides, I wasn't even sure a pastor could help me. I had been a fairly effective pastoral counselor myself for a few years, but I couldn't help myself.

The Internet had been my downfall, but now, I thought, it might help me find my solution. Back at my computer, I typed the words *sex addiction nashville* into the topic field of my favorite search engine and clicked. The results were stunning: a long list of twelve-step groups, workshops, retreats, treatment centers, and counselors with Nashville connections. *Entirely without realizing it, Allie and I had moved to the center of the world for sex addiction recovery!* I picked up the phone and called one of the two international twelve-step sex addiction recovery organizations based in Nashville and left a cryptic request for information on voice mail. A few minutes later my phone rang, and a friendly voice gave me the directions to a local meeting.

Predictably, the meeting was held in the basement of a church. I had always associated Alcoholics Anonymous, the granddaddy of twelve-step recovery programs, with church basements, and I had faithfully heeded my father's warnings to steer clear of any church where AA meetings were held. I knew my father's diatribe by heart. "No Christian needs to stand up in a meeting and confess, 'I'm Joe and *I'm an alcoholic!*'" Dad would tell his congregation. "You have a new identity! You can say, 'I *used to be* an alcoholic, but then I met Jesus! I *used to be* a sinner, but a transformation has taken place! I am no longer the man I used to be! I have been crucified with Christ, nevertheless I live—yet not I, but Christ liveth in me! I am now a new creation—old things are passed away, behold all things have become new!'"

With my father's words echoing in my ears, I arrived at the church ten minutes early and pulled into a space at the far edge of the parking lot, feeling like an apostate and a pervert. My palms were sweating. I picked up a book and pretended to read as other cars arrived: a battered pickup truck, a shiny Porsche, a minivan, a convertible. One by one, the drivers walked to the basement door and went inside. I kept watching as a few more cars pulled into the lot. A couple of drivers glanced in my direction, but I ignored them. Finally, fifteen minutes after the meeting's scheduled start, I took a deep breath and reached for my door handle. Suddenly I was struck by a thought. *It's rude to walk into a meeting late. I don't want to be rude. I'd better come back another time.* I started the car and drove away.

On my way home, I rehearsed the answers I would give Allie. Had I gone to the meeting? *Yes.* (Technically, that was true. I had gone *to* the meeting, I just hadn't gone inside the meeting.) What was it like? *It was good.* (Obviously true. If it wasn't good, other people wouldn't bother going to it.) What happened? *I'm not supposed to say.* (Also true. The members of twelve-step groups are anonymous, and the details of meetings are confidential.)

But when I got home, Allie didn't ask me about the meeting. She didn't mention it the next day either. She kept busy around the house, treating me with civility but keeping her distance physically and emotionally. A couple of times I caught her crying, but she wiped her eyes and refused to talk with me about it. "I'll get through this, thank you," she said.

Two days later I was back at the church parking lot, watching other guys walk inside. Suddenly I caught sight of a familiar face. I couldn't remember the guy's name, but I knew I'd seen him several times at a men's Bible study at church. He was not the leader of the Bible study, but he had joined freely in the discussions. A businessman like me, he had seemed strangely at peace with himself. He was not afraid to describe, in a matter-of-fact way, his own doubts and fears and failures. This guy seemed more interested in being honest than in impressing me or anyone else. I got out of the car and followed him inside.

My First Meeting

Downstairs in a musty room cluttered with boxes, a dozen folding chairs were arranged in a circle. I ventured toward an open chair opposite the guy from church. He nodded amiably in my direction, without a hint of recognition.

I cleared my throat. "Is this the . . . ?" My voice trailed off nervously.

"Rotary Club?" he asked.

"Uh, sorry." I turned to leave.

The guy grinned. "Relax. If you want the meeting for sex addicts, you're in the right place."

I blushed and sat down. *Sex addicts.* The term sounded dirty, shameful. *If you want the meeting for sex addicts*—No, I did not want the meeting for sex addicts. I wanted the Rotary Club, Promise Keepers, or Drivers Against Mad Mothers—anything but this.

A few guys stepped across the circle to welcome me. They shook my hand and told me their names, which I promptly forgot.

A balding young man opened a loose-leaf notebook and said, "Hello! My name is Joe, and I'm a sex addict."

"Hi, Joe!" said everyone else.

Hi, loser, I thought.

"Let's open this meeting with a moment of silence, followed by the Serenity Prayer."

We sat in silence, heads bowed. Somewhere in a corner of the basement, pipes gurgled. As if on cue, the group intoned, "God, grant me the serenity to accept the things I cannot change, the courage to change the things I can, and the wisdom to know the difference. Amen."

The meeting proceeded in an orderly fashion. Members took turns reading short selections aloud, informative little dissertations with titles like "The Problem" and "The Solution." I could feel myself drifting, but a few phrases landed in my brain like grenades. *We were addicted to the intrigue, the tease, the forbidden . . . Our habit made true intimacy impossible . . . Fantasy corrupted the real; lust killed love . . . First addicts, then love cripples, we took from others to fill up what was lacking in ourselves . . .*

"Do we have any newcomers?" the leader asked, looking in my direction.

"I'm just visiting," I said. "Checking it out."

He looked around the circle. "Who'll do the newcomer meeting?" The guy from church and two others raised their hands, then stood up and headed for the door. The leader motioned for me to follow them. I rose unsteadily, feeling doomed. *Dead man walking . . .*

I followed my companions outside to a pair of concrete benches under a tree. A lawnmower droned in the distance. The guy from church looked me straight in the eye. "Congratulations on getting this far," he said. "Most people never make it to the first meeting."

"Thanks," I said. "I'm just checking it out."

He smiled. "I don't know whether you're a sex addict or not, and that's actually not a diagnosis any of us can make. You'll have to draw your own conclusions. Right now, we'll just share some pieces of our own stories, and maybe you'll hear some things you recognize."

For the next forty minutes, I listened with astonishment as three strangers took turns describing my secret life. The details of our stories were different in many ways. Each man recounted some scenes of abuse or experimentation that were unfamiliar to me. Still, their inner lives—their emotional experiences and their perceptions of themselves and others—were almost identical to mine. The dawning realization that my problem was a common one was exhilarating and depressing all at the same time.

On one hand, I was not alone, and that was very good news. On the other hand, I was not unique. There was a term for guys like me— *sex addict*—and that was extremely disappointing. The bad news was now official: I was broken. I was a sex addict, and I would never become a man of integrity.

☠ five ☠

The Integrity of a Sinful Man

AFTER OUR OUTDOOR NEWCOMER MEETING, I RETURNED with my new friends to the basement room for closing exercises. The leader passed a plastic case to another guy, saying, "Bill, will you do the presentation of chips?"

Bill opened the case. "In this program, we use a chip system to commemorate periods of sexual sobriety," he explained. "We define sobriety as 'No sex with self or partners other than the spouse.'" He held up a small red plastic disc. "Is anybody celebrating thirty days today?" No one spoke. He picked up a series of other discs. "Sixty days? Ninety? Six months? Nine months? A year? Multiples of years?"

A man wearing a suit and tie raised his hand. "Three years," he said, and the room erupted with applause. Bill stood up, formally presented the guy with a metal coin, and gave him a big hug. Whistles and shouts filled the air.

"Tell us how you did it!" Bill said when the applause had died away. "What's your secret?"

The guy spoke softly. "I *didn't* do it. That's the secret. I hung around this program for years trying to stay sober, and it got me nowhere. I just couldn't seem to figure this thing out. I knew the principles worked for other people, but I couldn't get them to work for me. When I lost my job and my wife filed for divorce, I finally gave up. By that time I wasn't even sure a Higher Power existed, but I asked him to save my life if he was there. I said that if he would relieve my obsession with lust for just one day, I would do my best to serve others and follow the advice of my sponsor."

The man's eyes filled with tears. "God answered my prayer that day and the next day and the day after that. I can't believe I've been sober for three years already. I have a whole new life today, and God used you people to give it to me. Thank you."

Finally, Bill held up a white plastic disc. "This is our most important chip," he said. "We call it the Desire Chip, and it's for anyone who wants to try this way of life one day at a time. This chip does not commit you to this program, but it does commit us to you. Would anybody like a Desire Chip today?"

I raised my hand. The room applauded.

Afterward my new friend from church invited me to join the rest of the gang for dinner at a Chinese restaurant. I looked at my watch and winced. "I don't know," I said. "I've got a lot to do, and my wife is probably wondering where I am."

He pressed me gently. "C'mon. It'll be good for you."

The atmosphere in the restaurant was relaxed, the conversation jovial. I turned to my new friend, "Well, now that I've joined this outfit, what do I do first?"

"You get a sponsor."

"Is that Step One?"

"No, but your sponsor will help you take Step One and all the other steps too. Nobody can do this alone. If you're going to get sober and stay sober, you need a sponsor."

"Okay, will *you* be my sponsor?"

He smiled. "I'll tell you what—I'll be your *temporary* sponsor. I'll get you started, but you should probably look around awhile to see if there's anybody you connect with better than me."

Later as we were leaving the restaurant, my new sponsor said, "Wait here." He walked to his car and returned with two books. "Read these," he said, handing me a hardback copy of *Alcoholics Anonymous* and a paperback titled *The Twelve Steps and Twelve Traditions*.

"I'm not an alcoholic," I said.

"Doesn't matter. Addiction is addiction, and recovery is recovery. Our drug is different from theirs, but we can learn a lot from these people. Just substitute *lust* every time the books say *alcohol.*"

"Okay. Anything else?"

"Yes. When you get up tomorrow morning, kneel beside your bed and ask God to keep you sober for the day. Then call me."

Meeting the Alcoholics

I stayed up reading *Alcoholics Anonymous* that night until 2:00 a.m. In the morning, after kneeling beside my bed and asking God to keep me sober for the day, I picked the book up again. *I don't want to bother my sponsor,* I thought. *He's probably busy. I'll call him later.*

The day sped by. I devoured the book, almost finishing it by evening. As my excitement grew, I made several attempts to discuss it with Allie, but she resisted, retreating from me even further. Her skepticism was understandable. Allie had listened to hundreds of my soapbox speeches during twenty years of marriage, and she'd seen me "turn over a new leaf" countless times. She knew my excitement was sincere, but she was also well acquainted with my impulsiveness and lack of discipline, my proven inability to stick with anything for very long, and she wasn't about to be hoodwinked again. Allie had run out of hope. She knew my latest obsession would pass.

The next day I attended my first AA meeting. I was pretty sure I wasn't an alcoholic, but I wanted to see the fellowship described in the book firsthand, so I called the number for AA listed in the phone book. It turned out that the closest meeting was scheduled for noon in a church basement just a few blocks from my house.

I arrived at the room to find about fifty people already seated in a double circle. Someone was reading a selection from *Alcoholics Anonymous.* I took a seat against the wall. Looking around, I was surprised by the diversity of the group. There were roughly as many women in the meeting as men. Some of the attendees wore business attire; others looked like students, homemakers, or laborers on their lunch break. Most were Caucasian, but I could see a sprinkling of African-American, Hispanic, and Asian faces. They appeared to range in age from teens to seventies. One woman was holding a baby.

"This is your meeting," the leader said. "Does anybody have a topic?"

A young woman spoke up immediately. "I'm Colleen, and I'm an alcoholic."

"Hi, Colleen!" said everyone in the room.

"As some of you know, I slipped a couple of weeks ago, right after picking up my one-year chip. I guess I felt the need to celebrate." A few chuckles rippled through the room. "Anyway, it wasn't pretty. I told myself I could handle just one drink, but things got away from me real fast. I drank for three days straight. When it was over, I felt so ashamed of myself that I wanted to die. I felt too ashamed to call my sponsor or go to a meeting. I even felt too ashamed to pray.

"Fortunately, my sponsor called me. She asked if I'd been drinking and I said yes. I half-expected her to fire me on the spot, but she asked if I was okay and if I'd learned anything about powerlessness. Then she told me that the slip could be a good thing if it showed me that my version of the program wasn't working. I had been confusing abstinence with sobriety, and I had been doing all the work myself and taking all the credit. She said that the one-year chip had probably given me a false sense of security. I'd regarded it as a personal accomplishment rather than a gift from God, as some sort of proof that I wasn't powerless over alcohol anymore and that I could handle life on my own. That kind of crazy thinking made it possible for me to drink again.

"I'm very happy to be here in this meeting today, but to be honest, I'm confused and scared. I'm worried about slipping again, and I'm still unclear about some of the things my sponsor told me. What is the difference between abstinence and sobriety? What is God's part in my recovery, and what is my part? I would appreciate hearing some experience, strength, and hope from you all today. Thanks."

"Thanks, Colleen!"

For the next forty-five minutes, men and women took turns addressing the issues that Colleen had raised. They spoke simply and directly out of their own personal experience, describing mistakes they had made and lessons they had learned. Some stories were hilarious; others brought tears to my eyes. The level of honesty was startling, the wisdom exquisite. At the end of the meeting, everyone stood, held hands, and recited the Lord's Prayer.

My emotions were churning as I left the meeting. My spirit was uplifted, but at the same time I was angry—furious—that never, in more than forty years of church attendance, had I experienced the safety, the honesty, the genuine concern and mutual respect that I had seen displayed by this community of recovering drunks. Even though the name of Jesus had not been spoken during the meeting, I had certainly sensed his presence there, and I had heard more echoes of his teaching during the meeting than in any sermon I could recall. These people were failures and outcasts, just the kind of losers Jesus had preferred to spend time with during his earthly ministry, but their fellowship was far removed from the Christian mainstream, their meeting relegated to a church basement in the middle of the day. Something didn't add up.

In the ensuing months, I attended a twelve-step meeting almost every day. Finding a meeting that focused on sex addiction was my first priority, but I could always drop in on an AA meeting in a pinch. I purchased all the organization's approved literature, including its history books, and studied them religiously. When the opportunity arose, I attended a seminar presented by AA's archivist. I also obtained and reviewed material published by a number of AA's secular and religious critics.

Gradually I began to understand that AA had never actually been banished to the basement by the institutional church. No, AA went to the basement voluntarily, convinced that it must sever its formal ties with Christianity in order to fulfill its mission to alcoholics. Because so many active alcoholics have been wounded by Christians and are suspicious of the church, AA deliberately distances itself from institutional religion. AA believes that only by doing so can some sufferers be induced to enter the fellowship and start talking about spiritual things.

AA serves as a sort of side entrance to the church for many recovering alcoholics. Their tentative trust in a Higher Power eventually becomes a strong faith in Christ. Other recovering alcoholics, however, never make the Christian connection. Meanwhile, although most *practices* of AA reflect those of the early church, the gulf between the *doctrines* of biblical Christianity and the amorphous spirituality of AA can be disconcerting to some Christian alcoholics and addicts, and doctrinal difficulties have sometimes aroused the opposition of conservative Christian leaders.

My Integrity

As the months passed and I gradually learned the stories of other guys in my twelve-step circle, I was surprised to discover that many of them were Christians. Some had landed in recovery after failing spectacularly in church; others were new Christians who had come to faith through their recovery experience. I soon learned that nearly every church in town was represented in this quiet subculture of anonymous recovering addicts.

One day while shooting the breeze with one of these guys after a meeting, I raised the subject of the group's religious pluralism. I knew this guy was a devout Christian, a leader in his church, and I wanted to know how he handled the non-Christian aspects of the fellowship.

I raised the subject carefully. "I'm really glad to be in twelve-step recovery," I said. "For the first time in my adult life, I'm experiencing some victory over lust. I am beginning to see real change in my character. My world is opening up. My heart is coming alive. Even my wife is starting to notice the difference. God is very real to me these days, but on another level I'm also feeling a certain amount of discomfort."

He looked at me knowingly. "Spiritual discomfort?"

"Exactly. Even though I haven't been a very *good* Christian, I actually do believe that Jesus is unique. To me, he's far more than a sage or a prophet. He's the Savior—the Way, the Truth, and the Life—the one mediator between God and man. I also believe in the reality of sin and the necessity of the Cross. I believe we all need forgiveness, that God extends forgiveness to us by grace, and that we receive it through faith in Christ."

"I believe that too," he said.

"So it's really starting to bother me," I said, "that I can't say the name of Jesus in a meeting without getting funny looks. We discuss sickness in the meetings but not sin, progress but not redemption, the 'Big Book' but not the Bible. And it's obvious to me that some people in these meetings believe in a god who's far different from mine, a spirit that pervades the universe but is indistinguishable from it."

"And you find that threatening?" he asked.

"Unsettling," I said. "Our god concepts are contradictory. They can't all be right, and the first of the Ten Commandments leads me to believe that my God is a little touchy on the subject of other gods."

"If you'll read your Bible carefully," he replied, "I think you'll find that God has always called his people to fidelity, but he has also taken pleasure in extending his kindness to those outside the family of faith. That, in my mind, is the main message of the New Testament. It's the message that got Jesus into trouble at the end of Luke 4. If Jesus were walking the earth today, he'd have plenty of criticism for the church, but I don't think he'd spend much time denouncing twelve-step groups on doctrinal grounds.

"Also, if you'll forgive my saying so," he continued, "it seems to me that your faith is more intellectual than actual. You *say* that you believe in God and Jesus Christ, but some of the non-Christians in this group display more faith in God than you do. They actually trust him. The conduct of your life up to this point shows that you don't. So rather than waste any more time obsessing over *their* gods, I suggest that you focus on the idolatry in your own heart. Ask God to reveal the things you worship more than him, and set yourself to the hard work of getting rid of those things."

Ouch.

In a later conversation, the same friend pointed out that my idea of integrity was unrealistic and unbiblical, and that this basic misunderstanding had prevented me from experiencing the power and sweetness of the gospel. I had been trying to *be* God rather than *love* God, trying to reach a place where I merited God's mercy and really didn't need it anymore. My ambitions had been way out of whack. Yes, it is true, he said, that God wants men of integrity. But integrity is not perfection. It is not completion. It is not even purity of intention, something that, frankly, we are all incapable of achieving. Rather, integrity is a combination of *rigorous honesty* about my own condition and *humble faith* in the steadfast love of God.

I decided to follow my friend's example and concentrate on my own faith rather than the theology of those around me. I even worked on shaking up my religion a bit, making an effort to talk to God without using Christian buzzwords and listening for his voice in everyday conversations, including conversations with people whose religious credentials were questionable. I also picked up a copy of *The Message* (NavPress 1995), the popular paraphrase of the Bible written by Eugene Peterson, and started reading a few pages of it every day.

For many years I had viewed the Bible as a preacher's sourcebook, opening it only to follow a sermon or to prepare one of my own. But now, looking at the Bible from a new perspective, I began to see in its pages a sprawling story of love and redemption, peopled with flawed characters and pulsing with passion, a story in which, in the end, the only real hero is God. Captivated by the story, I resolved to read all the way through the entire Bible for the very first time. There, quite unexpectedly, I encountered myself in the story of Samson.

Part Two

I, Samson

☠ SIX ☠

Who Am I?

NanaNanaNanaNanaNanaNanaNanaNana . . . Batman!

Even though I never saw the television show, I knew the theme song to *Batman*. Everybody did. My school friends sang it loudly on the bus and in the locker room. Sometimes we all hummed it during study hall, and when old Mrs. Shoemaker, the proctor, angrily ordered us to stop, I'd look up innocently and say, "Stop what?" while the other tables kept humming. Eventually Mrs. Shoemaker would remove her hearing aids in frustration, and we'd be free to talk.

Batman and his superhero colleagues, however, were not allowed inside my father's house. Dad had no use for fictional messiahs flamboyantly attired in flowing capes and colorful tights. The only heroes he respected were real ones, Bible heroes. There was Jesus, of course, the ultimate superhero. There was also Samson, whom I first encountered in the full-page color illustrations of *Egermeier's Bible Story Book* (Warner Press, 1969).

In those pictures, Samson was the ideal man, striding through Canaan bare-chested, a housewife's dream. He had a fabulous physique, chiseled features, and great hair. Samson was invincible in battle and irresistible to women. By contrast, I was a skinny kid with glasses, very vincible in battle, and completely resistible to women. When my father closed the storybook and we all closed our eyes to pray, I sometimes imagined that I was Samson.

The Historical Samson

The real Samson was born in Palestine, late in the twelfth century BC, during a time when the fortunes of Israel had fallen. After their dramatic escape from slavery in Egypt two hundred years earlier, the Hebrews had reached the Promised Land and settled there, but their conquest of the land had eventually faltered, and now they were living under virtual military occupation. The pagan Philistines had gained the upper hand, an advantage they maintained with a strict policy of gun control. The Philistines made it illegal for Hebrews to own metal of any kind. Denied the raw materials for swords and spears, the Israelites were reduced to tilling their fields with wooden plows. Their crude clubs and arrows were no match for the glittering weapons and armor of the Philistines.

The Hebrews desperately needed a deliverer. Not that everybody wanted one. Many Israelites had compromised with Canaanite culture, adopting Philistine ways and even imitating Philistine worship. Some had intermarried with the Philistines and had given their children Philistine names. Still, a remnant of devout Israelites clung to the worship of their God, Yahweh, and cried out to him for rescue.

Samson arrived on the scene as a messianic figure, sent by God in response to the pleas of his people. An angel announced the good news of Samson's impending birth, first to his mother and then to his father. The angel instructed the prospective parents to consecrate their son with a special vow. When he was born, they obediently designated Samson a Nazirite. Never in his life would he enter a bar or a barbershop.

Samson grew up knowing he was special. His parents, who practically worshipped their son, indulged his every whim and excused his tantrums as the birthright of a gifted child. Samson reached manhood with the settled belief that he was unique, a demigod with a divine mission, someone to whom the rules that governed ordinary mortals simply did not apply.

When the time came for Samson to assume his role, he began

challenging the Philistines in very theatrical ways. Aggressive and highly confrontational, he went to elaborate lengths to goad Israel's well-armed enemies into battle. Once, we're told, Samson methodically captured three hundred foxes, tied them together in pairs, tied torches to their tails, ignited the torches, and set the foxes loose in the grain fields of the Philistines.

The Philistines were an agrarian people. Like Cain, their worship centered on the fertility of their fields. The pride of the Philistines was in their crops. Their god was Dagon, the god of grain. By burning the grain fields of the Philistines, Samson was attacking more than their livelihood; he was attacking their religion. The Philistines responded with fury. They invaded.

The Philistines offered the terrified Israelites one way out of the crisis. "Give us Samson," they said, "and we will let the rest of you live." Frantically, Samson's countrymen began looking for the young man. They found him relaxing in a cave at Etam. As a mob of Israelites surrounded the place, a delegation approached Samson and urged him to surrender. Samson obliged, calmly allowing them to tie him up and carry him to the field headquarters of the Philistine army. He arrived at the Philistine camp bound with new ropes, escorted by three thousand unarmed Israelites.

But when the Philistine commander approached Samson, something extraordinary happened. As the Bible puts it, "The Spirit of God came on him [Samson] with great power" (Judg. 15:14 MSG). Suddenly infused with supernatural strength, Samson snapped his bonds as if they were straw. Then he reached for the closest object at hand, which was the jawbone of a donkey. With that jawbone as his only weapon, he attacked and killed a thousand Philistines.

What a phenomenal feat! The news of Samson's astonishing victory electrified Israel and shot fear into the hearts of the Philistines. Israel's deliverer had come! Overnight, Samson became the spiritual and political leader of his people.

The Bible tells us that Samson enjoyed a long career in public service. For twenty years, he settled disputes among the Jews and administered their civic affairs while continuing to harass the hated Philistines. From all accounts, he was a competent and conscientious leader. The biblical record gives no indication that Samson ever failed in his professional duties. Outwardly, publicly, he was a success. But Samson's private life was a disaster.

During his teenage years, Samson had developed the habit of cruising alone through Philistine territory in search of adventure and female companionship. It was a dangerous game, one he should have given up when he became the leader of Israel, but by then he believed he was bulletproof. Samson always showed up for work in the morning, but when he clocked out at the end of the day, he often slipped away for some secret recreation.

There were a few very close calls during those years. To the Philistines, Samson was Public Enemy Number One, and they were always hunting for him. They planted spies, paid informants, and set ambushes for the reckless leader of Israel. More than once Samson barely escaped with his life. Any sane man would have heeded these warnings and stopped taking foolish risks, but Samson did not, could not. He was drawn to illicit excitement like a moth to a flame.

Then one day, when Samson was about forty years old, the wheels came off. He was spending an evening with Delilah, a pagan girlfriend who had already betrayed him three times. Blind to her schemes and beguiled by her beauty, Samson finally revealed to Delilah the terms of his Nazirite vow, which was the source of his great strength. Then, while Samson slept, Delilah cut his hair and called to the waiting Philistines. They overpowered the helpless hero, bound him in chains, and gouged out his eyes. Then they put him in prison, where they set him to work serving their god, grinding grain.

Years passed. His career over and his reputation lost, Samson now spent his days in absolute darkness, walking in circles. It was a pointless, monotonous existence, illumined only by regret.

But one day Samson's daily routine was unexpectedly interrupted. A Canaanite religious festival came to the city, a raucous celebration not unlike Mardi Gras. His guards led the shackled Samson out of prison and into a pagan temple that was packed with partying

Philistines. At the sight of their vanquished enemy, the crowd roared. Samson suddenly sensed an opportunity, one last chance to redeem his failed life and complete his mission. Helped by an unsuspecting Philistine boy, he positioned himself between two pillars that provided crucial structural support for the building. Looking heavenward, he breathed a prayer for help. Then Samson pushed the columns apart, and the building collapsed.

Samson died gloriously that day, taking more Philistines with him in his death than he had killed in his entire life. But even this achievement did not deliver the Israelites from their oppressors. The grip of the Philistines was not broken. Samson died without accomplishing his mission.

A Successor to Samson

At about the time Samson died, another messianic figure was born in Israel. This birth, however, was a quiet one. No angels heralded the arrival of Jesse's youngest son. The boy grew up in obscurity, unaware of his destiny. Not even his father suspected that David was the new deliverer until God revealed his identity to a visiting prophet.

Like Samson, David enjoyed spectacular episodic success against Israel's enemies. In fact, after he became king, David accomplished what neither Samson nor King Saul could ever do—he defeated the Philistines for good. David established a secure border for Israel and created a stable political state. He established a capital city. He brought the ark of the covenant to the city and led a revival of worship in Israel. Warrior, poet, musician, king—David was a tremendous leader.

But when he was about forty years old, the wheels came off. The collapse happened suddenly. One day, as he was looking over the bustling city from the rooftop of his palace, David caught sight of a neighbor woman taking a bath. Overcome by desire, he found a way to meet her. Their affair developed with dizzying speed. Almost overnight, David found himself doing things that Samson had never done, committing adultery and then covering up that sin with murder.

After the Collapse

Samson and David—two great men, two great failures. But after they failed, the lives of these two men moved in opposite directions. Samson spent his last years alone, in bondage and blindness, and he died a failure. David, on the other hand, recovered. His collapse was a bitter experience, but he emerged from it a wiser man and a better king. David died a success, surrounded by friends and family, and he left a legacy.

Why the difference? Why did one man recover while the other man did not?

I now believe that David recovered *because he could*, and Samson didn't recover *because he couldn't*. David recovered because he had learned to do the things that make recovery possible. Samson never learned to do those things.

What things am I talking about? Well, consider with me these four distinctions between the two men:

Distinction One: Isolation vs. Companionship

The Bible is a storybook, a stirring saga of love and war, tragedy and triumph. What makes this story so compelling, so enduring, is that it is true. The characters in the Bible are real people, and the Bible describes their strengths and weaknesses with unflinching honesty.

Samson is a major biblical figure. His life spans four entire chapters in the book of Judges, and he dominates every scene in which he appears. Samson's performances are so strong that the typical reader doesn't notice the utter absence of a supporting cast until someone points it out. *Samson was a man who never bothered to make friends*. Aside from his parents, the Bible gives us the name of only one person who ever got close to him: Delilah.

In this respect, David's life was markedly different, but it did not start out that way. David was a precocious child, so competent and self-sufficient that his father soon sent him into the fields alone to guard the flocks that comprised the family fortune. There, far away from the bickering of his older brothers, David found peace. His only audience was God. Beneath the open sky, he could sing at the top of his lungs. In glorious solitude he could spend hours in target practice without a word of correction or ridicule. True, the idyllic life turned monotonous at times, and the tedium was occasionally punctuated by moments of sheer terror. But David grew to believe that with God's help he could defeat any threat single-handedly.

David's world changed completely, however, on one momentous day—the day he killed Goliath. That was the day David made his first friend. That was the day he met Jonathan.

It was really Jonathan who made the famous friendship possible. Its formation defied political logic. As the oldest son of the current king, Jonathan was the rightful heir to the throne. Nobody would have criticized him for identifying the handsome young giant-killer as his greatest rival, a threat to be contained and neutralized. But when they met, Jonathan did a remarkable thing. The Bible says that the prince took off his armor and belt (his personal defenses) and gave them to David. Then he took his offensive weapons, his sword and his bow—*things David could hurt him with*—and he gave those to David too. Having made himself completely vulnerable, Jonathan offered his hand to David in friendship. They formed a covenant that day—a pact that saved David's life on more than one occasion, a promise that outlived them both.

His friendship with Jonathan set a new pattern for David's life. Having made one friend, he went on to make hundreds more. "Every man who was desperate, in debt, or discontented," the Bible says, "rallied around him, and he became their leader" (1 Sam. 22:2). The names and descriptions of David's friends go on for pages. While King Saul, consumed by jealousy and paranoia, was raging against his advisors and driving his best warriors away, David befriended the weak and the strong. He eventually counted among his most trusted friends men whose military exploits were even greater than his own. David surrounded himself with giant-killers, and he learned to listen to them. Together, he and his friends accomplished what no one man could have done.

When Samson fell, he fell alone, surrounded only by enemies. When David fell, he fell among friends. It was those friends, especially one courageous, godly man named Nathan, who made his recovery possible.

Distinction Two: Rover vs. Homebuilder

The book of Judges portrays Samson as a man perpetually on the move. Never one to waste time sitting at home, Samson relished the freedom and anonymity of the road. Closed doors and locked gates could not contain him. He preferred the easy company of strangers to the suffocating sameness of family and friends. Samson always kept an eye on the exits, and he came and went as he pleased. In scene after scene we see him traveling far from the beaten path, usually somewhere in enemy territory, always alone.

In his post-Jonathan days, David was different. While he did travel at times—like most of us, he could scarcely avoid it—only rarely did he travel by himself. In road scenes we usually see David at the head of a throng or within a cluster of fellow travelers.

When he was given the choice between heath and hearth, David generally preferred to stay home. The first thing he did after establishing Jerusalem was to build a house for himself there, a fine, comfortable house suitable for raising a family and entertaining friends. In fact, David was home, relaxing on his own rooftop patio, on the day he fell.

Samson was far away from home when his world collapsed. When the cold, hard chains encircled him and the darkness fell, Samson didn't call out for help, because he knew there was no one within earshot who cared.

David, when he fell, was at home. Even as he tumbled headlong into a private hell, David could still see his friends, and his friends could see him. And though he was too weak and confused to call out for help, his friends could see that he was in trouble, and they came to get him.

Distinction Three: Reflex vs. Reflection

Samson was a true action hero—a doer, not a thinker. He was the strong, silent type (which is another way of saying that he was emotionally constipated). Samson didn't second-guess himself. He didn't bother analyzing his motives or agonizing over his mistakes. He knew that his problems were caused by other people, mostly those damned Philistines, and that the best way to deal with them was to respond with overwhelming force. Samson believed his only security was in strength. He didn't like to show weakness—not to God, not to other people, not even to himself.

It's interesting that of all the scenes from Samson's life described for us in the Bible, only one contains a prayer. Samson was the spiritual leader of Israel for twenty years, but he was not a man of prayer. He had more important things to do. His only prayer recorded in the Bible was a final, desperate plea for strength before his spectacular suicide attack at the Philistine temple.

On this point, the contrast between Samson and David could hardly be more striking. The book of Psalms, the longest book in the Bible, is a treasury of transcripts from David's daily conversations with God. In these prayers we see David's passionate relationship with the mysterious Power that overshadowed his life. The relationship was a real one, and like every relationship in which a human being is fully present, it spanned the whole range of human emotions.

On some days David was almost giddy with excitement, completely secure in God's affection and tender care. Praise poured from his lips like a waterfall, and he sang of faith and trust and confidence.

On other days, however, David's words sound to us like voice mail left by an estranged lover who has had too much to drink. Bitter and angry, he complained that God was impossibly far away, indifferent to his troubles or, worse, was the very cause of them. At times he sank into self-pity and despair. At other times he admitted feeling afraid or ashamed, besieged or embarrassed, conceited or confused.

Whatever his mood, David was invariably honest with God, and he was usually honest with those around him. Though he was committed to self-examination, he knew that he would never discover the darker hollows of his heart without the help of God and others. He was not afraid to appear weak, because he understood that all flesh is weak. He did not try to appear perfect, because he understood that all flesh is flawed. He also believed, at the deepest level, that he belonged to God, and that God is strong and perfect and, above all, good. Rooted in a genuine relationship with God, David lived his life, all of it, out loud. And he left his honest prayers behind for the rest of us to echo.

Samson, the determined strongman, was severely handicapped by a voluntary blindness. He was sightless long before they took his eyes. Samson walked straight into an obvious ambush at Delilah's house, the same house where he had been ambushed on three earlier occasions, and yet he never saw it coming.

David made the mistake of staring into the dazzling fire of lust one day, and he was temporarily blinded by it. But his sight was soon restored, *because David really wanted to see*.

Distinction Four: Big Plays vs. Little Plays

Samson and David were both aware that they had been given an enormous mission. To deliver Israel—that was no ordinary assignment. The very fact they had been chosen to do it proved that they were not ordinary men. Indeed, both men were gifted in phenomenal ways. What separated them was not their level of giftedness but their style of play.

Samson considered himself a home-run hitter. He was larger than life, a franchise player, and he was swinging for the fences every time he came to the plate. Whatever the situation, Samson always believed that he was just one spectacular play away from final victory. He never bunted. He never thought small. Who but Samson would catch three hundred foxes?

Samson began his career in the big leagues by killing a thousand Philistines in one day. David, on the other hand, began his career by killing just one—but David killed the right one. From that point on, David's battle against the Philistines was a team effort, and his team eventually won.

Samson never lost hope that he could turn things around on his own. Even when he was standing in the middle of that Philistine temple, blind and shackled, pelted by the taunts of his enemies, the old delusion returned. Suddenly Samson was seized by the sensation that he was three runs down in the bottom of the ninth, with the bases loaded and the count full, and that with one massive blow he could deliver a miracle come-from-behind victory, redeem his failed life, and fulfill his destiny. It was not to be. He set a record for Philistine-killing that day, but when the dust cleared, Samson was dead and the Philistines were still in charge.

David faced a similar temptation at the end of his life. He was looking back over his career one day, reliving all the old campaigns, when a magnificent idea suddenly appeared. With one final flourish, he could atone for all his failures and secure his reputation as a man of God. Samson had ended his life by destroying a temple; David would build one! He would build the world's most beautiful temple for the God of Israel. That would be his legacy.

With great enthusiasm David took the idea to God. And God shot it down. "Here's what I want you to do instead," God said. "Prepare your son to build the temple. Give him everything he will need to do it. Devote your remaining days to being a godly father, and you will leave legacy enough."

I, Samson

Having narrowly survived a bone-jarring, head-snapping collision with my own depravity, it suddenly occurred to me that my childhood fantasy had come true. *I was Samson*. Yes, I was a man with a mission. Yes, I was gifted. Yes, I had produced a few impressive accomplishments. From all outward appearances, I had been a competent professional and a mature Christian. But inside, I had been a desperate fugitive from reality, bound for blindness and self-destruction. Isolation, which had always felt safe, had really not been safe at all.

I was Samson. To survive, I needed to learn how to live like David.

☠ seven ☠
Walking Lessons

IN THE EARLY STAGES OF MY RECOVERY JOURNEY, I SOMEtimes went for days without calling my sponsor. The truth was, I didn't really want help—not *human* help. I wanted *God* to help me, without involving anybody else. I am, after all, an American male, a rugged individualist by temperament and training. I am also an evangelical Christian. (It's no accident that America's favorite hymn insists "I come to the garden *alone*, while the dew is still on the roses.")

I was willing to trust Christ, but I was not ready to trust the body of Christ.

To be honest, even my confidence in Christ had worn thin. Evangelists and pastors had promised that all my problems would be solved by a personal relationship with Jesus. I had been reaching out for that relationship for almost my whole life, and where had it gotten me? My biggest problem had grown progressively worse, until I was a lying loner hooked on porn and prostitutes. By the time I hit my bottom, even my wife didn't like me anymore.

Of course, my relationship with Jesus had never been quite what the preachers described, not even after I became the preacher. The nagging awareness of my religious hypocrisy had prompted countless silent promises to do better. I had vowed to spend more time with God, get up earlier, pray longer, and memorize more Scripture. I had made these promises in good faith, but I lacked the discipline to follow through on them for more than a few days, and I felt terrible about that.

My personal relationship with Christ hadn't worked, and I knew it was my fault. What I did not yet understand was that while Jesus does offer a personal relationship to every one of his disciples, he never promises any of us a *private* one. Jesus first said, "Follow me" to two men, not just one, and to those two he quickly added ten more. Later, when he sent the disciples out to represent him, he sent them out in pairs. Finally, as he was preparing to depart from this earth, he promised his followers that he would still be present with them, but under very clearly defined terms. "Whenever *two or three of you* are gathered in my name," he said, "I'll be there" (see Matt. 18:20).

The church, according to the New Testament, is not a loose confederation of individuals. The church is a body—a living, breathing organism whose members are so intimately connected that they can only move *together*. On any given day, every member of that body needs help, and every member has some help to give.

For years I had been begging God for a private solution to my private problems, and he had always ignored that request. Sometimes, in my more despondent moods, I had concluded that he didn't respond because he didn't exist. At other times I had interpreted his silence as proof that he didn't care. Mostly, however, I had continued to believe that some precondition for his kindness was still unmet, that if I would just ask properly and behave nicely and really, *really* believe, then he would give me the relief I sought.

Of course, God does not always grant relief to his daughters and sons. He certainly didn't give the apostle Paul relief from his painful "thorn in the flesh," whatever it was, even though Paul begged with tears on multiple occasions for God to take it away. God's response was, "No, Paul, I like you better with it. That thorn is a faithful reminder of your humanity. Without it, you would foolishly try to take my place. With it, you remain weak, and my strength is perfected in weakness" (see 2 Cor. 12:7–10).

Considering Paul's problem and God's response, I was suddenly struck by the possibility that God's apparent inaction in a painful area of my life might have been deliberate. Maybe, just maybe, God knew I needed that problem. He hadn't afflicted me with it, that was clear, but maybe he loved me too much to take it away. Maybe that problem was the only lever in my life big enough to force me out of my determined isolation and into honest relationships with other members of the body of Christ.

I had not gone to my first twelve-step meeting willingly, that's for sure. I had been driven there by my problem. And on that day one man—the man who would become my first sponsor—did a brave and beautiful thing. He took off his armor and gave it to me. Then he took his spear and his bow—things I could hurt him with—and gave those to me too. He told me, frankly and in considerable detail, about mistakes he had made in his own life. He also talked about a change that had occurred, although he was careful not to describe it as a cure. He spoke of his sin in the present tense. Life is a journey, he said, and he offered to walk with me awhile.

On that day, I had made my first male friend since childhood. In the months and years that were to follow, that friendship would become the first of many.

Learning to Call

I wanted the friendship my new sponsor offered, but for some reason I still resisted it. At our second meeting he reminded me that I hadn't called him yet. "Try to call once a day," he said. "Call more than once a day if you need to. Call any time you start feeling crazy, any time you find yourself slipping toward the edge. And in between those times, just keep me updated about what's going on in your life."

Despite my sponsor's kindness, I found it excruciatingly difficult to pick up the phone and call him. I did manage to call on a semi-regular basis, but before long I was giving him edited versions of my progress, omitting or minimizing any troubling thoughts or worrisome behavior. Within two months the old behavior had returned. Too embarrassed to admit it, I stopped calling him altogether.

This first relapse was demoralizing. When I finally got around to telling my sponsor about it, he smiled and said that the crash was inevitable. After all, I hadn't really made any deep changes in my life yet. I hadn't asked or answered the hard questions or accepted any unpleasant advice. I hadn't started the Twelve Steps. That fabulous feeling that felt like sobriety had actually been a novel form of intoxication, a temporary euphoric state that is so common among recovering addicts that they have given it a name: "The Pink Cloud." But my "pink cloud" had dissipated. Reality had reasserted itself, and I was going to have to get serious about doing the real work of recovery if I really wanted to change my life.

After thinking about what my sponsor had told me, I concluded that I must have chosen the wrong sponsor. This guy was well-meaning, but I found it impossible to trust him, and I was certain that the problem was *his* rather than mine. I needed to find someone else. By this time I had met plenty of very impressive guys in the twelve-step meetings I was attending, including several doctors and a few ministers. I finally approached a college professor after a meeting and asked if he would be willing to become my sponsor. "Sure," he said, handing me his card. "Call me."

I really wanted to impress the new guy, so I called him every day for about a week. First I'd formulate some snippet of insight, then I'd rehearse it, and finally I'd make the call. He wasn't fooled. "What is it that you *don't* want to tell me?" he'd ask. "Tell me that." After dodging this question a few times, I stopped calling him, and soon I was back on the Internet again, downloading porn and feeling worse than ever. I decided the problem was simple. I needed a new sponsor.

My next target was another guy from church. After semi-confessing my latest relapse at a meeting, I approached him privately and asked if he had time for another sponsee. "Sure," he said. "Here's my number. Call me."

A couple of weeks later I encountered him in the hallway at the church, and he asked me how it was going.

"Not good," I admitted. "I'm having a hard time."

"I'm sorry," he said. "Who are you calling?"

I juggled my Bible and said, "I'm calling God, but he doesn't seem to be answering."

"Really? That's too bad." He smiled. "May I suggest something? The next time you decide to call God, call me. Call God by calling me."

To my religious ears, his suggestion sounded profane. *Did this guy think he was God?*

He checked himself, as though reading my mind. "Not that I'm God or anything," he said. "Lucky for both of us, I'm not. But God does speak to me through other people, and I'm fairly confident he's able to speak to you through someone like me."

The habit was a hard one to acquire, but I gradually learned to make that daily telephone call. And that's when my turnaround really began. Looking back, I mark the beginning of my recovery from the day I finally surrendered to the discipline of picking up the telephone each day to share the truth about my life with another guy and ask for his honest feedback. Dialing was excruciatingly difficult at first, each digit a mockery of my supposed self-sufficiency. But forcing myself to make the call brought enormous spiritual benefit. With each conversation I surrendered a little more to the reality of my place within the human race. Today I understand (most of the time) that I am a man among men. I need my brothers and my brothers need me.

Nowadays I routinely make two or three calls each day to trusted men within my circle of friends. I call when I'm feeling irritable or discontent, afraid or alone, depressed or euphoric. I call when I'm faced with a difficult decision or when I feel a wild urge to do something self-destructive. And most of the time when I make that call, God answers. The voice belongs to a human friend, but as we talk I can feel the presence of someone else. Personally, I believe that Jesus is there, in the person of the Holy Spirit, honoring his promise to be with us, even to the end of the age.

These days my phone routinely rings a dozen times a day with similar calls. The conversations are usually brief—we're guys, after all—but a few minutes of verbal honesty seem to unleash an unworldly power in our lives. At those times when I cannot answer the phone, the caller will usually leave a detailed message on my voice mail. Whether I actually call him back is not the point. After all, I'm not the fount of all wisdom. He is not really calling me. He's calling God, and God always listens. For those of us who spent years resolutely steering our lives from one ditch to another, one of the most practical ways to surrender to Christ is to pick up the telephone and tell the truth to another Christian. God always rewards that simple act of humility, even if we wind up spilling our guts to a machine.

Learning to Stay

With the help of my sponsors and friends, I gradually made fundamental alterations to the way I live my life. For one thing, I gave up my roving and decided to settle down.

My roving instinct is deeply rooted. I wandered a lot when I was single. I drifted around college, around the country, and around the world—almost always alone. I loved to surprise my "friends" by showing up somewhere unexpectedly, joining them for a few laughs, bragging about where I'd been and where I was going, and then taking off again. My best stories were largely bogus, of course. I entertained my audiences with fictionalized accounts of actual events, the exciting parts embellished and the shameful parts removed. Between shows, I endured long stretches of loneliness. Sometimes, as I shouldered my way through a crowded market in some strange city or watched the sun fall behind some distant mountain, I had ached for a wife to share the experience. *As soon as I get married*, I remember thinking, *this loneliness will end.*

It's ironic that I carried the habit of roving into my marriage. Let me be clear on this point. I love my wife. I have always cared about her in my own fractured and incomplete way, and I have cared about our children too. But for many years there was something about the company of anyone, even someone as extraordinary as Allie or as precious as our kids, that made me want to cut and run after a while. No matter where I was, I felt the need to get away.

I fled into work and ministry, but even there I never stayed in one place for very long. I gravitated toward jobs with little daily account-ability, sales jobs and executive positions. My only full-time job in the ministry was as a pastor, a position I took when I was just twenty-five and quit when I was thirty. That congregation trusted me to use my time responsibly, and I regularly abused their trust. My greatest invention was my official schedule, jam-packed with long pastoral calls and hours of study. Mostly I played around.

As the years passed, the pattern grew worse. My family and my busi-ness associates began referring to me as "the phantom." Sometimes as I was leaving the house, my youngest son jokingly asked if I was going to spend time with my "other family." I'd grin and say, "Yeah, buddy. Off to see my other little boy."

Truth was, I didn't even enjoy my own company. I dreaded silence. In the car, I reached instinctively for the distraction of the radio. Unwilling to think about my own shortcomings, I obsessed over sports and politics. Afraid to face the present, I spent my time spinning elabo-rate fantasies about the future or compulsively reliving the past. And like the prodigal in his flight from home, I sought the approval of strangers as a substitute for love.

But now, with the encouragement of my new friends, my life slowly started changing. Not *everything* has changed—I still sometimes drift away during conversations, for example, and I tend to leave parties early—but generally I am present in my own life. I enjoy the company of others, and I spend my days openly, among family and friends.

Evenings and weekends I'm with Allie, and we often find a way to meet somewhere in the middle of the weekday for lunch or exer-cise. My mornings follow a comfortable routine: an early walk through town followed by personal devotions in a local coffeehouse, and then work. Fortunately, there are several public places in our little town where I can write, places with broadband access and an open table.

My weekly schedule includes several standing appointments with other men I've grown to trust over the last few years. We'll meet for coffee or a sandwich at our regular time, and after a little small talk we'll get down to sharing what's really going on in our personal lives. These guys know my story, and I know theirs. We have spent so much time listening to each other that we can now recognize recurring patterns of thinking and behavior, and we rely on each other for feedback. My friends challenge me. They hold up mirrors for me, offering glimpses of parts of my life I would probably never see on my own. They tell me things about myself that Allie might never say.

When my work requires me to travel, as it does from time to time, I try to take someone with me, preferably Allie or another person in recovery. If I absolutely must travel alone, I file a detailed "flight plan" with Allie and a few of my friends, and then I do my best to maintain regular radio contact while I'm gone. I call from the car, from the airport, from the lounge, from the rental counter, from the lobby, from the room. I arrange to meet people where I'm going. These are things I never did during my roving days, back when I worked hard to keep my schedule loose and my itinerary as vague as possible.

Finally, I've learned not to travel alone through cyberspace. As a rule, I only go online in public places. I've also installed a monitoring program on my computer that automatically e-mails my Web history to a friend who will call me immediately if something suspicious turns up.

> Prone to wander, Lord I feel it.
> Prone to leave the God I love.
> —"Come Thou Fount of Every Blessing"

I still feel the tug of the road sometimes. No matter how sweet the comforts of home, how bracing the camaraderie of friends, my pride still campaigns for self-sufficiency and my faulty memory sometimes complains that life was better when I was out there on my own. When my closest relationships are in turmoil and I'm facing the painful prospect of rejection, I find myself missing that me-and-Jesus religion that promised so much and delivered so little. My friends have taught me that it is best, in those times, to take my feelings to God, but to do so by putting them on paper and saying them out loud the way David did.

A Life of Reflection

My first sponsor gave me some great advice when I was getting started on this road to recovery. He told me I should eat well and exercise, and go to bed at a decent hour. He told me that way I would be able to get up in the morning and spend a little time in prayer, study, and reflection before plunging into work. He also recommended that I begin journaling.

I had started countless journals through the years, and every one of those efforts had fizzled after just a few pages. Resolving to do better this time, I bought a fancy leather-bound book and a fine pen, and then I found a quiet place where I could sit and record my thoughts for posterity. On the first day I wrote two pages. On the second day I wrote one page. On the third day I wrote a paragraph, and then I didn't pick up the journal again for a week.

The next time my friend raised the subject, I described my failed attempt and told him that I didn't think I was capable of journaling on a regular basis. He laughed.

"You're writing for publication, aren't you?" he asked.

I reacted defensively. "No, I'm trying to express myself clearly on paper. And I'm being careful, because someone may read it someday."

"So you're writing crap."

"No, I'm writing good stuff, but it takes a lot of work."

"You mean you're writing *good* crap. That's the worst kind."

I looked at him helplessly.

"Look," he said, "try this. Go to the discount store and buy a spiral notebook and a cheap pen. Tomorrow morning, sit down and write three pages without lifting the pen from the paper. Write as fast as you can. You should finish in about twenty minutes."

It sounded impossible. "What should I write?" I asked.

"Write what you feel."

"But what if I don't *know* what I feel?"

"Then write what you think you *might* feel if you weren't such a freakin' nice guy. And when you're finished," he continued, "tear those pages out of your notebook, wad them up, and throw them away."

Journaling became easy when I followed his directions. I gradually learned to be honest on paper as the weeks passed. Freed from the need to perform and protected from the fear of exposure, I watched the most amazing things come out of my pen. Some of them were ugly and some of them were beautiful, but each one made me feel a little more alive.

I quickly came to appreciate the value of this kind of writing, its ability to break the cycle of obsessive thinking. If the world were divided into "thinkers" and "feelers," I would certainly be counted among the thinkers. My first instinct, whenever I encounter a challenge of any kind, is to try to think my way through it. Problem is, I tend to think in circles. My untethered thoughts spiral upward into grandiosity or downward into despair. I *think* I'm thinking, but in reality my brain is merely chattering crazily to itself. But when I *write*, I write in straight lines. After pouring out my feelings for a few weeks, I was surprised to find that my journal was actually taking me somewhere.

Other friends and sponsors introduced different elements into my journaling time. After I had learned to be honest, someone suggested that I start addressing my journal to God, speaking to him out of my true heart as David did. Someone else recommended that I take some time each day to read a short selection from the Bible or a healthy devotional book, listening for God's voice. That person also urged me to compose a gratitude list every day.

In the first chapter of his letter to the Christians in Rome, the apostle Paul offered a chilling description of humanity's descent into depravity. The apostle said that the slide toward all-consuming lust begins when we refuse to acknowledge that God is God, and we are not grateful (see Rom. 1:21–32).

I had learned to express my thoughts and feelings honestly in my journals, and that was a very good thing. I was saying out loud what I had been thinking all along. But there was danger here too. If I wasn't careful, I could easily become an inveterate whiner, nursing my grudges and rehearsing my complaints day after day in my writing. I could turn into one of those cynical, self-obsessed bloggers who clog the Internet. And it wouldn't stop there, because when I'm feeling deprived I tend to throw civility aside and seek compensation. For me, it's a very short trip from deprived to depraved.

I've found that the best way to keep from going down that slide again is to write a gratitude list every day. The list serves to remind me that I have not been neglected by Providence. That's a fact I tend to concede lightly when I pray, quickly saying something like, "Thank you for all your blessings" before getting down to the real business of begging God for more. But when I stop, actually stop, and take a few minutes to list some of those blessings in detail, the magnitude of God's goodness begins to sink in. He may not have indulged my every whim, but God has surely been extraordinarily kind to me. My life may not be perfect, but it is extremely good. I may not have everything I want, but in many ways I am already rich beyond measure.

When I begin with gratitude, the trajectory of my journaling and praying is elevated from complaint to confession. I may still express all kinds of negative emotions to God, but when I am grounded in gratitude I can do so without blaming him for them. Remembering the many ways God has cared for me in the past, I find it easier to believe that he will remember me today. And when I see how many of my blessings have been birthed through pain, I gain the hope that today's pain, however meaningless it appears, is working toward a redemptive purpose.

Faithfulness in Small Things

The grandiosity of Samson has marked my life for as long as I can remember. Deep within my DNA, apparently, lies the conviction that I have been put on earth to do huge things, spectacular things, and that by virtue of my destiny I occupy a privileged place above the common run of humanity. It's an attitude that expresses itself in strange ways, such as a reluctance to stand in line and wait my turn, or fill out forms, or follow rules. Rules, after all, are for ordinary people, and I am a special case. My grandiosity has little regard for the schedules of others and is therefore chronically late. It loves to talk. It hates to listen. It instinctively manipulates every situation to achieve its own ends, and does so shamelessly.

Oddly enough, I am also prone to bouts of self-loathing. During these moods, my accomplishments seem paltry in light of my potential, and I am mocked by the successes of others. I become one of those double-bound wretches, an egomaniac with an inferiority complex—what my friends laughingly call "the piece of crap the universe revolves around."

These are the two faces of pride, and both of them cajole me to greater effort. They tell me I must justify myself by doing more. They say that I must get more at-bats and that I must hit the ball harder and farther. I must do great things for God.

My friends tell me something different. They remind me that I am merely part of a team. I am unique, they say, but only in the way that every snowflake is unique. We are different, but not easily distinguished. We are all composed of the same stuff. We all fall to the ground, and we achieve our most captivating beauty in community.

When I listen to the stories of my brothers, I find to my surprise that they are telling my story too. A friend shares his weakness, and I am strengthened by it. Another shares his experience, and it fills a hole in my own. As my ego deflates and I take my rightful place within the created order, I feel the joy that comes from living as a worker among workers, a man among men.

Lately I have been dreaming that I am a bricklayer in a vast and fabulous city. The walls and buildings of the city have been rising for centuries, and millions of workers are engaged in the ongoing construction. My friends and I are laboring at the corner of a building, where we are constructing an ornate arched doorway. When it is finished, the arch will serve as an entrance to the building and a support for the stories above it. We work patiently and carefully, savoring the joy of our shared purpose as the doorway slowly emerges.

I love that dream.

The dream, I think, is true. The city of God is being built, and it is being built one brick at a time. A game with a child. An honest conversation with a friend. An evening with a spouse. A phone call. An admission. An apology. A disclosure. A small fidelity.

One brick at a time.

Part Three

A New Way of Life

⚑ eight ⚑
The Rebirth of the Real Me

EVERY SUMMER, THE CHURCH I ATTEND PRESENTS A WEEK-long Vacation Bible School for kids. It's a preadolescent extravaganza, staffed by hundreds of adult volunteers. I have been evading the program's recruiters for years.

In June of last year a woman whose name I did not recognize when it came up on the Caller ID finally cornered me. She sounded desperate.

"I'm calling about Family Bible Adventure," she said. "I need help."

"Hang on. I'll get my wife."

"I need a man."

"Excuse me?"

"I'm looking for a man to play Adam in the Garden of Eden, and two people on the committee suggested you."

"Me? Adam? Are you sure?"

"Pretty sure, yes."

"Have you ever *seen* me?" I asked. "I'm not exactly the Adam type."

"Yes, I've seen you. And you'll be playing Adam *after* the Fall, so you'll be fine."

"I'm awfully busy," I said.

"It will only take ninety minutes a day."

"I don't have any time to learn lines or rehearse—"

"You won't have any lines. I'm playing Eve, and I'll do all the talking. You're basically a prop. Up until yesterday my husband was going to be Adam, but now his company is sending him out of town for the whole week."

I bit my tongue. "I don't have a costume," I countered lamely, grasping for an excuse.

"No problem. The costume is already made. I'll bring it with me."

So for the next week, wearing a rugged nightie that made me look remarkably like Fred Flintstone, I stood for ninety minutes each day beside a gurgling fountain on the church lawn, surrounded by potted plants, listening to a Tennessee mother tell the story of Adam and Eve to clusters of small children. She told that story over and over and over again.

Once we lived in a beautiful garden . . .

I watched the children as she spoke, and after a while I noticed something. Most of the children had been raised in church and had obviously heard the story before. But there were also quite a number of unchurched kids, neighbors and playmates who were attending the program with their friends. These kids had never heard the story before—but still, *they didn't seem surprised by it.* It was almost as though they *recognized* the story somehow.

I suppose there is within all of us, somewhere at the cellular level or deep in the collective unconscious, the memory of a paradise lost. We half-remember a beautiful garden, perfect love, meaningful work, leisurely evenings that seemed to last forever, and we are dimly aware of a tragic misjudgment and a sickening crash that brought it all to an end. As we look around in the twilight, we know that things were better at one time than they are today, that *we* were better. For all of us, the story of the Fall is a *personal* story.

The apostle Paul spoke about the story in intensely personal terms. "I was once alive, apart from the law," he wrote wistfully to the Romans. "But when the commandment came, sin came alive and I died" (see Rom. 7:9–10). Paul said that he did not come to life again for years, not until the day he stumbled into Damascus a broken man, blind, and almost born again.

Persona Non Grata

Only God can create a real person—a *complete* person, body, soul, and spirit—but God has given each of us the ability to create personalities. Sometimes a child who has been subjected to severe emotional or sexual abuse will use this God-given ability to create multiple personalities, independent *personas* that hide from each other. Most of us merely use this power to develop a sort of interior theatrical troupe, whose members take turns at center stage.

One day during my midtwenties, I was fiddling with the radio in my car when I bumped into a motivational speaker addressing a large crowd. He was telling his audience how to get a better job. "You need to go into that interview with *confidence*," he declared with great confidence. His voice dropped to a whisper. "Are you *afraid* to go in there and compete for the job? Well, I have a solution for you." He paused for a moment and then shouted, "Don't go! Send somebody else! Figure out what kind of person they want to hire, then *create* that person and send *him* to the interview!" The room erupted with applause.

I followed his advice and found that it works. I am capable of creating a convincing alter ego, a persona, and that false self can get a job quite easily. It's just hard for a persona to *keep* a job. Sooner or later, people catch on.

I've actually gone to church on mornings when the sanctuary was full and none of the members were there. Everyone had sent somebody else. Heck, I've usually sent somebody else to do the preaching.

I was an adolescent when I first realized I am not always the same person, that there are several versions of me who appear and disappear in response to my surroundings. In those early days, the cast included Church Nate and School Nate, Home Nate and All Alone Nate, and they were definitely different people.

The first time I laid eyes on Allie, we were in church. I was home from college. She was a brand-new believer, radiant with the beauty of newfound faith. I promptly introduced her to Church Nate, and she fell in love with the guy. Church Nate can be quite charming, and he showed a chaste concern for this new sister in Christ. Before long she found herself imagining a lifetime with him, serving the Lord together and talking every day about God.

A year later I introduced her to Date Nate. That encounter did not go nearly as well. Allie thought Date Nate was a jerk. Personally, I liked the guy, but I reluctantly sent him into exile and brought in Mate Nate instead.

After we were married, and School Nate and Church Nate went off to seminary, Mate Nate more or less disappeared. Allie couldn't figure out what had happened to him. She still misses him sometimes.

Later, when I left the pastoral ministry and went into business, I developed a new persona: Mag Nate. His job was to develop business for the engineering company, and he sold himself beautifully. It was exhausting work, though, and despite his success, Mag Nate was burned out in just a few years.

That's the biggest problem with personas. A false self can never rest. It *looks* like a real person, but a persona is actually just a hologram, a projected image, and it requires constant energy to keep that image up. A persona is afraid to go to sleep, because to sleep is to die.

Also, because it has no inner reality, a persona must always be focused *outward*. It must always be scanning the audience, responding to the whims of the watchers, adapting to their shifting moods.

A persona is hollow, and is therefore plagued by a constant empty feeling. It may try to fill that inner void with any number of things—applause, excitement, food, sex, romance, knowledge, money, just to name a few—but the emptiness never goes away.

The religious persona is probably the most tragic figure of all, because it recognizes spiritual realities that it can only pretend to experience. A persona can perform, but it cannot love. It can know excitement, but can never experience joy. It can feel numbness, but it can never know peace. A persona can be persistent but not patient, subtle but not gentle, sweet but not good. It can feel fervor, but it can never know faith. It can be modest but not humble. It may starve itself by sheer force of will, but a persona can never achieve self-control because *it has no continuing self*.

The biblical word for *persona* is *flesh*. And the Bible makes it plain that no matter how spiritual or religious it appears, flesh is always hostile to God. It may mimic righteousness. It may feign repentance. But flesh cannot see God, cannot know God, and cannot love God. And it cannot worship God, because God is Spirit, and those who worship him must worship him in spirit and in truth.

The Rich Young Persona

Mark wrote about Christ's encounter with a desperate young man (see Mark 10). Jesus was about to set out on a journey, Mark said, when a well-dressed young man ran up to him, threw himself at his feet, and cried, "Good master, what must I do to inherit eternal life?"

Several people standing around recognized the young man right away, for he was a prominent local personality, a leader in the religious community. The young man was very good at being very good, and his life was marked with the kind of success that religious people usually associate with virtue.

But despite his outward prosperity, the young man did not feel alive. He felt empty, numb. He had been impressing audiences for years, but he knew that his life was a sham. He had constructed a successful persona, but he was dead inside and he was desperate to find real life.

Jesus responded to his question in a very odd way. Cocking his head, he said to the young man, "Good? Why do you call me *good*? No one is good but God alone."

Jesus then reminded the young man about the unyielding biblical standards of goodness. "You know the commandments: 'Do not kill. Do not commit adultery. Do not steal. Do not lie. Do not cheat. Honor your father and mother.'"

Despairingly the young man said, "I've followed all these rules from my youth—*and I'm still dead!*"

Mark said that Jesus looked at the young man and loved him. Gently he said, "Then here's what I suggest. Leave this audience. Close the show. Sell the stage, the costumes, and the props and *follow me* on a great adventure."

The poor young man couldn't do it. He had become too obsessed with building his own goodness. For too long he had been keeping the rules and making up more, thinking that if only he were *right*, if only he could *do* all the right things and *learn* all the right things and *get* all the right things and *say* all the right things, he could bring himself to life.

Jesus was saying, "*It's not about being good! It's about being! God* is good, and that is good enough." Jesus was inviting the young man to join him and his disciples on a journey. He was inviting him to place his trust in a goodness not his own, to abandon his pious, false life in order to find his real one.

The poor young man couldn't do it.

A Conversation After Dark

The apostle John, in the third chapter of his gospel, described another famous encounter between Jesus and a persona. John said that a religious leader named Nicodemus sought a private audience with the teacher. He showed up after dark at the place where Jesus was staying, slipping in through the back door to avoid being seen. After all, Nicodemus had a reputation to protect. He was very good at being very good. He was widely regarded as a religious expert, someone who had his life together, and he could not afford to be seen seeking answers. *But Nicodemus was empty inside, and he was desperate for something real.*

Nicodemus approached Jesus respectfully, nodding to him as one professional to another. Folding his hands and clearing his throat, he said, "Rabbi, we know that you are a teacher sent by God, for no one could do the signs that you do unless God were with him."

Jesus got right to the point. "Unless a man is born again", he said, "he cannot see the kingdom of God." His meaning was clear. Jesus was addressing a persona, a hologram who was dead inside, and he was telling Nicodemus that his only hope lay in the miracle of rebirth.

Nicodemus protested. He wasn't dead. You could ask his mother.

Jesus said, "What's born of the flesh is flesh. What's born of the spirit is spirit. You think you're a grown-up, Nicodemus, but you have never even lived. You are dead. Your present self is only flesh. Your present life is something you made up. Your spirit, the *real* you that God knew before the world was made, is dead, and it needs to be reborn" (see John 3:6–10).

We don't know how he responded that night, but John wrote that Nicodemus was eventually counted among the believers in Jerusalem. When the religious police were seeking to arrest Jesus, Nicodemus came to his defense, and after the crucifixion, he helped prepare Jesus's body for burial. He was surely there on that glorious morning three days later when Jesus rose again, fulfilling his promise to return to life a people who had been dead since Eden.

A Tale of Two Selves

So what happens after a person is reborn? What is that person's new life like?

Well, I know what my life is like today, and I can tell you that it bears a strong resemblance to the life the apostle Paul described in chapter seven of his letter to the Romans. Most of the time I have at least two selves. Only one of these selves is real, but they both *look* real and they both *act* real.

My true self, the one God made and miraculously brought to life again, is immature and unsteady, but he is growing stronger all the time. He is fully alive, and his life is marked by spiritual reality. He experiences love, feels joy, and knows peace. He is growing in patience, showing gentleness, acquiring kindness, and displaying faith. He is learning humility, and he is developing self-control.

But this new self, my true self, is not alone. At any given time, he is opposed by at least one false self, a persona I created long ago, an aging actor who loves the stage and does not yield it willingly.

To use Paul's language, these two are "spirit" and "flesh." The practice of the Christian life, he said, consists of learning how to follow one and forsake the other, trust one and distrust the other, listen to one and ignore the other. This is not as easy as it sounds, because flesh is devious and very persistent.

It doesn't help, I guess, that most of my false selves grew up in church. They can speak the lingo. They know the songs by heart. Although they are certainly capable of debauchery and unspeakable cruelty, they are also very good at being very good, and they are determined to regain control of my life.

My false selves abhor the thought of surrendering to God or God's people. They insist that I was only sick, not dead, and that I can still recover on my own. They also ridicule the idea that God really loves me.

My false selves warn me that childlike faith in God's goodness is naive, that simple trust in his patience and care is insane. God expects me to shape up, they say, and quickly too. His forgiveness expires. He has not really set me free, but has merely placed me on probation. God has given me a push, they say, a boost, a second chance, but now it's up to me to get my life together and make it to the finish line.

My false selves beat the drum of self-improvement while chanting mock encouragement. *Work hard! No mistakes! You can do it! We can help!*

"*What?*" Paul asked, aghast. He was writing to the Galatians, but he was also talking to me. "Are you *Crazy?* Are you actually thinking of letting *them* run your life again? *Why?* They are *dead*, and everything they produce is dead. There was a time when you were dead too. Do you remember the futility of your old way of living, the frantic performances, the emptiness after the show? Why would you go back *there?*"

Paul was right.

The road ahead does not run through improvement of the old self but through acceptance of the new one, the *real me*. I am *finding* a life, not constructing one. I am doing things prepared beforehand, fulfilling an eternal purpose. The real me—the one God created at the start—is alive again, as spiritually alive as Adam was before the Fall. I am alive, and I am not alone.

Finding My Voice

There are some wonderful advantages to this new way of living, this lifestyle of walking by the spirit. For one thing, it's simpler than walking by the flesh. That's not to say that it's *easier*—at least not in the early stages. My old way of slogging alone through life was hard work, very hard work, but I had grown accustomed to it. Living by self-propulsion had come to feel natural to me, natural and necessary. It had seemed right. This new life of faith, on the other hand, feels very unnatural at times, awkward and frustrating. Learning to live this way is like learning to ski, only harder. I still fall down a lot.

But there are those times, between spills, when I find my balance and feel the pure joy of grace. I am acquiring a taste for this kind of movement, the glorious sensation of being carried along, rushing toward life in all its beauty, respecting its dangers but not fearing them, leaning into it, holding my center, relaxing, sensing myself being held upright and borne upward—until self-confidence overcomes me and I swerve into a tree. I have learned not to ski alone.

I have also learned that my true self is naturally talented. The "real me" already possesses gifts and abilities my wannabe false selves fruitlessly cultivated for years.

For example, I have been a public speaker since high school, but I was never satisfied with my voice. It always sounded strained, and I usually started going hoarse after about thirty minutes in front of a crowd. I worked very hard at improving my speaking voice, buying books and tapes and practicing with a tape recorder, but my efforts only seemed to make matters worse. Allie pointed out that I used an "important voice" when I got up to preach. She said it sounded artificial, and I knew she was right, but I just could not get the hang of making myself sound natural.

This problem was particularly vexing because it hampered my

dreams of working in radio. After one humiliating experience, a local radio interview in which I came off sounding like Barney Fife, I finally abandoned that dream and decided I would become a writer instead. But the writing didn't go any better. I started a dozen best-selling books, agonizing over each line, writing and rewriting, and abandoned them all because they sounded like nonsense.

When my carefully constructed life finally came crashing down, the crisis forced me to set those ambitions aside and focus instead on breathing. My new friends kept me afloat. With their encouragement and guidance, I started facing and accepting the truth about what I'd done and who I'd tried to be. As I took that ugly truth to God, approaching him in simple faith and giving it to him in pieces, I started noticing an internal change. A new "me" was emerging. I was beginning to live from the inside out rather than from the outside in. I was learning to *be*.

A few years passed. One day, out of the clear blue, somebody asked if I would be interested in narrating a radio show. Surprised, I said yes. I went into the studio braced for the worst, but the session flowed almost effortlessly. Before long I was being offered voice-over work on a fairly regular basis.

A few days ago, I was sitting behind a microphone in a recording studio, narrating a film about the 2008 Beijing Olympics and listening to myself on a set of padded headphones, when suddenly the miracle struck me. The voice I was hearing was the voice I had always wanted, the one I had been looking for all my life, and here it was, coming from somewhere deep inside me of its own accord, flowing out of me like water.

The same is true of this book. For the past year, my friends have been urging me to write this stuff down, and I have declined. I didn't think I could do it. I thought it would be excruciatingly difficult, like all those other times. And yet here I am, putting the truth about myself on paper, and it is flowing out of me like water.

☠ nine ☠

Call No Man Father

WHEN MY DAD LEFT HOME AT SIXTEEN, HE WAS DETERMINED to be different from his old man. My grandfather, a former pastor who had dropped out of church completely, gave the boy ten bucks and wished him luck. Dad didn't own a suitcase, so he built a box from scrap lumber, put his few possessions inside it, threw the box over his shoulder, and started walking toward the state road. It was cold, and he didn't have a coat.

Dad arrived at his destination—the Bible college—with nothing more than the contents of that box and a burning desire to serve God. The school's founder, a farmer-turned-preacher who was known around the campus as "Pop," took a look at the earnest young man and said he could stay.

For the next three years, Dad performed all kinds of jobs around the campus in exchange for tuition, room, and board. He also worked as a soda jerk at the sandwich shop downtown and did odd jobs around Shorty's Ford garage. But Dad's favorite thing to do was follow Pop around, soaking up everything he said.

As the thirteenth of sixteen kids, Dad had grown up without much personal attention from his father. But now someone else's old man was filling the void. Pop took my dad and a few other young guys—a gang of ruffians who became known as "Pop's boys"—along with him on short jaunts and long trips. He identified and affirmed my father's gifts, gave him a worldview and a philosophy of life, and taught him about subjects as diverse as animal husbandry and prophecy, horticulture and divine healing.

Oddly, Pop's relationship with his own son, Carlton, became a little strained. They remained cordial, but Carlton, who succeeded his father as head of the Bible college and served as its president for decades, found other mentors. He listened to his father's advice, but Carlton also took the counsel of some cultured and sophisticated fellows Pop privately disdained. Pop spent the last few years of his life in quiet retirement, tending the fruit trees behind his house, and my dad remained fervently loyal to the old man until the day he died. Years later, during one of those wrenching controversies that follow revival as surely as night follows day, Dad cut all ties with the Bible college, saying, "Pop would never have tolerated what's being done here today."

The Sounds of Patricide

When I was a little kid, I believed my dad was the tallest man in the world. It was an easy mistake to make, since he towered over my mother (she was only four foot nine) and much of his public life was spent on a platform, preaching to the upturned faces of his children in the second row. I was shocked, frankly, when I returned from college to find that my old man was actually an ordinary guy, medium height, medium build, not much different from me.

By then my view of my father had changed dramatically in other ways as well. No longer was he the all-wise expert on spiritual matters that I had imagined him to be. He seemed, instead, like the survivor of an earlier, more primitive age, hopelessly out of touch with the wider world of biblical scholarship and comparative religion that I was discovering in college.

At about this time, his church entered a period of explosive growth, and Dad became a celebrity in regional religious circles. Soon he was surrounded by a group of disciples, earnest young men who hung on his every word. Some of them told me they envied my position as his oldest son, but they were hopeful that as his "spiritual sons" they too would find the help and guidance they were looking for.

Dad did help those guys. Never hesitant to delegate responsibility, he ordained dozens of them to the ministry and sent them out to plant and pastor churches. Within ten years he was commanding a formidable army of active church workers, and some people were jokingly referring to him as "the Pope of the North Country." His position seemed unassailable, his legacy secure.

But then in a stunning overnight reversal, Dad was unseated from leadership in the church he had founded, replaced by a younger guy, one of his protégés. No scandal precipitated the coup; Dad's behavior had always been above reproach. But looking at it from a distance and listening to the various accounts secondhand, it seemed to me that a shift in perception had occurred, a sea change in perspective among his spiritual sons. As a spiritual father, the old man had not lived up to everyone's expectations. Some people said he was too narrow, too dogmatic and dictatorial, that he didn't listen well enough, and he was starting to repeat himself.

Dad did his very best to remain gracious after the coup, but he struggled with feelings of betrayal. His shock and confusion were not unlike the sentiments Julius Caesar expressed moments before he was assassinated. (In case you've forgotten, the death of Julius Caesar conveniently cleared the way for his adopted son, Caesar Augustus, to assume the post of emperor.) According to the Roman historian Suetonius, Julius's last words were not "*et tu, Brute?*" as Shakespeare would have us believe, but a plaintive "*kai su teknon?*"—Greek for "You too, my child?"

So I'll Be the Daddy

I spent my college and seminary years searching for a surrogate father, sizing up dozens of candidates and eventually rejecting them all. Plenty of intelligent and gifted men crossed my path, to be sure, and a few of them even expressed an interest in helping me, but my standards were very, very high. And even though I desperately wanted an older man to look up to, I carried an equally powerful hostility toward authority, a seething suspicion that compelled me to criticize and antagonize every decent prospect.

Finally, when I turned twenty-five, I decided that I was old enough to be the daddy. That's when I started a church—or, to be more precise, I assumed the leadership of a disgruntled group that had already left a big church. Technically I was a co-pastor, partnering with an older guy who had served on the staff of the aforementioned big church, but the older guy recognized my ambition to be the "lead dog" and pretty much let me run things. Eventually he resigned, and the church became all mine.

I loved being "the man" in that church, ruling our little "family" as seer and sage. Even though I was practically the youngest adult in the congregation, I slipped quite naturally into the father role. Soon people twice my age were coming to me for advice and sitting in rapt silence while I taught. Elders and deacons lined up to support almost every course of action I proposed. Eventually some folks grew weary of the routine and drifted away, but they always did so quietly. Nobody ever challenged me directly.

In a way, pastoring was sort of like "playing house" for me. I was acting like a grown-up in public every week, even though I still felt like a kid inside and was usually acting like one when I was alone. The church game was rather fun, and everybody else seemed to be enjoying it. Everyone knew the rules and understood their roles. Obviously there could be only one daddy in the family, and that was me. Occasionally a catfight would erupt as a pair of women battled for the role of mommy, but the rest of the members obediently followed along, falling into their "child" roles with scarcely a word of complaint.

Even the language of our church supported the parent-child paradigm. In the doorway after Sunday service I would often hear, "I came to church this morning hoping to be fed, and you didn't disappoint me, pastor. Thank you." I liked it when people appreciated the hard work that went into cooking up a good sermon and serving it with style. To be honest, it never really bothered me that I was the only one doing the cooking and serving, nor did it occur to me that by spoon-feeding my people year after year I was keeping them trapped in perpetual infancy.

I also failed to recognize the true nature of the psychological control my paternalistic position gave me in the church. By accepting the role of father I was essentially declaring myself to be a benevolent dictator, offering security and care to my parishioners in exchange for grateful dependency and quiet obedience. It's the same strategy that political dictators have employed cynically and deliberately throughout history, usually with great effectiveness. In Russia, for example, "Our Father the Tsar" was replaced by . . . Father Lenin. The Emperor Hirohito maintained the loyalty of his people during a suicidal war against America because he was the "Father of Japan."

Other twentieth-century strongmen—Nicolae Ceausescu of Romania, Marshall Tito of Yugoslavia, Fidel Castro of Cuba, "Papa Doc" Duvalier of Haiti, and Charles "Pappy" Taylor of Liberia— exploited the father image to maintain the fealty of their people. Cult leaders have adopted the same strategy—"Father" Jim Jones and Charles Manson of the Manson Family come immediately to mind. And in literature, Ernest Hemingway, a peerless practitioner of the Cult of Personality and a renowned control freak, named himself "Papa" while he was still in his thirties.

On a conscious level, I certainly nurtured no intentions of becoming a dictator in my church. On the contrary, I was vocally committed to participative leadership. I tried to build teams, but for some reason the teams almost always fell flat as soon as I walked away from them. And to make matters worse, I was eventually stalked by potential followers, earnest young men (and a few women) who desperately wanted me to "disciple" them. These were nice people, but their potential for ministry seemed paltry in comparison with mine, and the idea of allowing them into my private world was abhorrent to me. I kept them all at arm's length. Politely, of course.

You Are All Brothers

Most of my preaching in those days was topical, focused on one provocative issue or another, but when I ran out of good topics I would sometimes announce an expository series. One such series took us through the Gospel of Matthew over the course of several months. I don't remember much about those sermons. I certainly don't recall how I handled the passage in chapter twenty-three where Jesus warned his disciples against adopting the leadership style of the scribes and Pharisees:

> But as for you, do not be called "Rabbi," because you have one Teacher, and you are all brothers. Do not call anyone on earth your father, because you have one Father, who is in heaven. And do not be called masters either, because you have one Master, the Messiah. (Matt. 23:8–10)

When I was a young father, I considered myself a pretty good parent. Today, however, the wisdom of Christ's warning stands out starkly to me, because I am painfully aware of the many ways I failed my kids, neglecting their deeper needs and squandering precious opportunities to love them well. I tend to apologize to my kids a lot these days, trying to make amends. They roll their eyes when I get started. "You're being too hard on yourself," they say, patting my arm. "We had a good childhood. You and Mom were great parents." But I can't help thinking, *I hurt you more than you realize.*

Because no human parent is perfect, every one of us is wounded during childhood, whether we recognize it or not. In ways big and small, the injuries inflicted by our parents impair our vision and restrict our movement, and our reactions against them produce all kinds of self-sabotaging impulses. Most of us start noticing our parents' imperfections during adolescence, and soon we are seeking surrogates among our peers or in popular culture. We may also look for that perfect teacher or perfect boss, an all-wise and all-caring adult who can explain the universe and show us our place in it. On some level, we're all looking for Pop.

But in the end, every one of our replacement parents disappoints us, because no human parent is perfect. Eventually we may decide to tackle the job on our own, to "parent ourselves," and we may try to salve the pain of our childhood by becoming a parent to others. If we have any aptitude for the role, it's fairly easy for us to attract disciples. Lots of people are looking for a surrogate parent. Inevitably, however, we disappoint all our followers to some degree. As our faults begin to show, our disillusioned disciples may drift away in search of better parents, revert to orphan status, or decide it's time to assume the parental role themselves.

Jesus's warning to us is startlingly clear. *Don't play house! Don't play school!*

Jesus always said that he lived his life in full view of heaven, constantly conscious of his Father's gaze, trusting his care and seeking only to do his will. Jesus taught his disciples to pray to "Our Father who is in heaven," and to trust their heavenly Father to meet their daily needs. He also promised that after his own earthly teaching ministry had come to a close, the Father would send his Spirit, the "Spirit of Truth," to indwell his people and lead them into all truth. "You have a Teacher," Jesus said. "And you have a Father. Therefore, do not expect any man to fill those roles, and don't try to fill them yourselves. Remember, you are all brothers" (see Matt. 23:9–11)

Washington or Bolívar?

The practical wisdom of the brotherhood principle is clearly illustrated in the contrasting careers of two political pioneers: George Washington and Simón Bolívar. Washington, of course, is revered in the United States as the father of his country. Bolívar tried to duplicate Washington's success in South America, but failed.

On December 23, 1783, George Washington made the greatest

single statement of his long political career by resigning his commission as commander in chief of the Continental army. This simple act of humility stunned the Western world. Washington, who had almost single-handedly held the fractious colonies together during the Revolutionary War, was easily the most trusted man in America. Grateful throngs called on Congress to proclaim him king. Other voices begged Washington to set up a military regime, believing that only a commander of his stature could create the stability necessary for a successful transition to democracy. Washington refused them all. Instead, in the scene powerfully recorded by John Trumbull in his famous painting, he traveled to the state house in Annapolis and surrendered his sword to the Continental Congress. Then he went home to Mount Vernon.

But that wasn't the end of Washington's career. Four years later he played a leading role in the constitutional convention in Philadelphia, and in 1789, the new Electoral College unanimously elected him president.

Washington discharged his duties brilliantly, operating as the consummate player/coach. Well aware of his own limitations and unthreatened by the genius of others, he surrounded himself with men whose intellectual talents were greater than his own, men such as James Madison, Thomas Jefferson, Benjamin Franklin, Alexander Hamilton, Aaron Burr, and John Adams. Compelled by the force of Washington's example, these men harnessed their competing egos and worked as a team. (Five years after Washington died, Burr killed Hamilton in a duel, but that's another story.) This team, the one that Joseph J. Ellis has called "the Founding Brothers," succeeded in doing what no one man could ever have accomplished, establishing the most durable republic in history.

As it turned out, George Washington became "the father of his country" by *refusing the role*.

In 1783, the same year Washington resigned his commission at Annapolis, Simón José Antonio de la Santísima Trinidad Bolívar was born in the Spanish province of Venezuela. By age nine, he was an orphan. By 1799, the year Washington died, the passionate young man had become a firebrand for liberty, forcefully arguing that the South American colonies should declare their independence from Spain.

When he marched into Caracas at the head of a liberating army in August of 1813, Bolívar accepted the title of "liberator" from a grateful populace and assumed political dictatorship. He went on to lead successful revolutions against Spanish rule in Ecuador, Colombia, Peru, and Bolivia. In fact, he served as president of two different countries during his lifetime, Colombia and Peru. When Upper Peru was liberated in 1825, the new nation named itself Bolivia in his honor. Bolívar personally drafted a constitution for his namesake, proposing a weak legislature and a strong president chosen for life.

By this time, Bolívar's power extended from the Caribbean to the border of Argentina, but his rule was not peaceful. The nations he had founded were wracked by a series of revolts and civil wars. On September 25, 1828, a group of young officers invaded the presidential palace and tried to assassinate him. The attempt failed, but more plots followed as competing generals jockeyed for power. He was denounced everywhere. Finally, in May of 1830, Bolívar agreed to leave South America and retire to Europe. He never made the trip, however. He died of tuberculosis six months later in Santa Marta, Colombia.

Despite his giftedness as a military commander, Simón Bolívar failed miserably as a political leader because he was never content to be a brother. He always needed to be the daddy. Although he employed the language of team play in his speeches, his actions showed that he never really trusted anyone but himself. In the end, it was all about Simón. It's no coincidence that the nations he founded are plagued by political instability to this day.

Decision Time

Because I was slow to accept the help of others, I relapsed often during the early stages of my recovery. My new friends didn't force me to accept their help, but they didn't give up on me either. Their doors were always open. After each confession they affirmed my courage and called me to a deeper level of honesty, humility, and trust.

Bit by bit, as I continued to attend meetings, make phone calls, and work and rework my way through the Twelve Steps, I came to terms with the world and myself. As I did, my destructive sexual compulsions gradually subsided. I could still feel the tug of temptation from time to time, but the urges lost their power when I shared them with my friends. Through countless meetings and conversations, those friends imparted to me the principles of *positive* sobriety, teaching me to live collaboratively and demonstrating a simple set of spiritual tools for maintaining freedom.

With each passing year, I came to believe the gospel a little more. *There really is a God. He really does love me. Jesus really has solved the problem of my sin, and he is working today through the community of his people. I really am a restored son of the sovereign Lord.*

The most powerful proof of God's existence was the transformation that was taking place in my character. As I identified my defects and surrendered them to God, I could feel myself becoming progressively less self-centered, less defensive, less resentful and afraid. I was becoming more honest, more loving, more fully present in my own life and the lives of others. Allie saw the changes too, and she gradually gained confidence that they were real. She slowly started trusting me again. That trust formed the foundation for the healing of our relationship, but plenty of work still lay ahead.

With my urge to isolate now in remission, I began spending a lot of time in public, hanging out in coffee shops and engaging strangers in friendly conversation. Gradually, as I got to know people and openings presented themselves, I started sharing my story with other guys. I was careful at first. If the time seemed right, I'd casually mention to a man that my life had been a real mess but it was getting better. If he seemed interested, I'd give him a few details, talking generically about addiction and some of the lessons I was learning. If he pressed the issue, I'd bring up the subject of lust. I found that most men I talked to were not sex addicts—they had not pursued lust to the degree I had—but every one of them understood my story and related to it in some way. If a man shared a part of his own story with me and asked for help, I'd offer to walk with him for a while.

I eventually disclosed my story to my pastor and gave him permission to pass my phone number along to anyone he thought I might be able to help. Before long I was receiving cryptic phone messages. "I talked to Pastor Scotty about something today," an unfamiliar voice would say, "and he suggested I talk to you. Do you have time?"

My friend Mike O'Neill, an addiction counselor and a recovering alcoholic, had told me that all addicts share an inner architecture, a common web of attitudes and beliefs that can manifest in a wide variety of compulsive behaviors. People with matching addictions relate most easily, but what helps one addict will probably be helpful to another, even if their addictions are different. Armed with that knowledge, I soon found myself in helping relationships with workaholics and alcoholics, food addicts and compulsive spenders. I was surprised to learn that even guys with no identifiable pattern of addictive behavior would want to spend time with me. Most of them had been living in isolation for a long time. They may have only been *potential* addicts, but they could feel the Philistines coming, and they saw a freedom in me that they wanted for themselves.

My circle of acquaintances grew wider. Some guys drifted away, but others soon took their places. Within a few years I was meeting one-on-one with about a dozen men each week and talking with many more by phone. Most of these friends did not belong to any twelve-step group, either because they weren't addicts or because they hadn't found a recovery setting they felt comfortable in. I loved dispensing wisdom to them, giving them hope, and making a difference in their lives.

Eventually, however, I started feeling a little uneasy about my role. Guys were looking up to me. I liked their attention. I liked being needed. But even though I harped on the theme of "rigorous honesty," I noticed one day that I had fallen into the habit of exaggerating my successes and downplaying my struggles. The realization shook me. I mentioned it to Allie and she agreed; I was on dangerous ground.

I had never told any of my friends' secrets to Allie—she didn't even know all their names—but now her curiosity was aroused, and she pursued the issue with all the skill of a federal prosecutor. "These guys you talk with every day, do they all know each other?" she asked.

"No," I said. "They all know me."

"Do *any of them* know each other?"

"Yes, some of them do."

"Do any of them call each other, or do they just call you?"

"I think they just call me."

"Why?"

"Because I asked them to. I'm helped by helping them."

"Do you tell them to call each other?"

"No."

"Would it help these guys to help someone else?"

"Yes, I'm sure it would."

"So why haven't you told them to call each other?"

"It never occurred to me."

"And why do you think it didn't occur to you?"

That was a very good question, and the answer seemed obvious. I didn't encourage guys to call each other because I believed that I was the one with the answers. I was the daddy. And now it seemed that I was willing to compromise my own authenticity in order to protect the prestige of my position.

Later that day I started talking with a few of my friends about forming a true mutual aid society, a group of Christian men who would live their lives together openly as equals, playing as a team. The idea resonated with each guy I spoke to.

A few of us got together to discuss the concept further, and the outlines of the group started to emerge. We would focus on forming fraternal relationships and facilitating a lifestyle of personal repentance. Our outfit would not be a *recovery* group exactly, because it would include both addicts and potential addicts, guys who had become aware of the dangers of isolation and wanted to escape them. Unlike classic twelve-step meetings, where the religious pluralism can inhibit some Christians from fully integrating their faith with the experience, our meetings would be designed specifically for followers of Jesus. To help maintain that distinction, we would retranslate the Twelve Steps, appropriating the principles that AA had borrowed from the Bible and rephrasing them in an effort to recover them for the church. And in another departure from classic twelve-step thinking, our group would not segregate its members according to their sins. We would try to take this trip together.

Pastor Scotty had just invited me to fill the pulpit at Christ Community Church on an upcoming Sunday morning, and I was preparing a message on the subject of male isolation. The stories of Samson and David were fresh in my mind. Tossing around possible names for the new group, I toyed briefly with "the Society of David," but that name sounded pretentious and a little pretty—too much like Promise Keepers. "How about the Samson Society?" I suggested. *Perfect.*

Within a month, we had gotten started.

My Father, My Brother

Every January I receive a minister's license in the mail, a sealed wallet card signed by my father, certifying that I am ordained to the gospel ministry and licensed by New Testament Fellowship of Watertown Inc. to preach for the current year. It usually arrives in a business envelope, wrapped in a plain piece of paper or enclosed in a form letter from a church secretary.

This year a small envelope arrived. It was addressed to me in my father's spidery hand, and inside along with the license, I found this handwritten note:

Dear Nate,

    I guess this is the first time I have ever written just to tell you that I love you. Your ministry is an inspiration to me. I have made many mistakes in my life, but I am proud of you and I pray for you every day. Please pray for me too.

Love,
Dad

Suddenly, my eyes filled with tears and I felt a great wave of affection for my father. I imagined him sitting at his kitchen table to write that note, spelling out my name, saying on paper that he is proud of me and asking me to pray for him. In that moment my father no longer seemed like a distant figure, and his weaknesses seemed inconsequential. In that moment he was a man writing words of encouragement to another man. He remains my father, to be sure, and I am still his son, but at that moment I could see that a change is taking place. The world is turning, and we are becoming brothers.

Part Four

The Pirate Monks

☠ ten ☠

The Adventure Begins

THE VERY FIRST OFFICIAL MEETING OF THE SAMSON SOCIETY convened on Monday evening, February 16, 2004, in the Women's Parlor of Christ Community Church in Franklin, Tennessee. It was a little weird at first.

"The *Women's Parlor?*" each guy had asked when I invited him. "Our church has a *Women's Parlor?*"

"Yep. They showed it to me. It's upstairs in the administrative wing, down the hall from the boardroom. We'll meet there at seven."

"But why there?"

"I don't know. Dr. McCurdy recommended it because it's quiet and private, I guess. And the boardroom is already being used."

As thirteen of us sat tentatively on rocking chairs and flowered sofas, surrounded by lace and needlepoint, I could sense the restraining presence of femininity in the room. The very air, redolent with potpourri, admonished us in dulcet tones, "Be nice." But we were not there to be nice. We were there to be real.

I distributed copies of the proposed Samson Society charter, a one-page document that I had been working on with Bruce McCurdy, director of the church's counseling ministry. (Scotty Smith and George Grant had also reviewed the earliest versions of the charter, offering feedback and encouragement.) This version was stamped "8th Draft."

"Before we get started," I said, "I'd like to propose a protocol for this meeting, a simple way of taking turns that will also help us learn each other's names. It goes like this: If you want to say something, begin by stating your first name, like this—'I'm Nate.' When the rest of the room recognizes you by name ('Hi, Nate'), the floor is yours. No one will interrupt you while you are speaking. The floor is yours for as long as you need it, but please keep in mind that the meeting is only an hour long and we want to give everyone an opportunity to speak. When you're finished, say 'thanks' or 'that's all,' and the rest of the room will acknowledge your contribution, thanking you by name ('Thanks, Nate'). Got it?"

Everybody nodded.

"Sounds like an AA meeting," said Bernie.

"Hi, Bernie," said Mark.

"I'm sorry. Was I supposed to say my name first?" Bernie asked, looking in my direction. I nodded.

"Sorry. Okay, I'm Bernie."

"Hi, Bernie," said the room.

"As I was saying, this sounds like an AA meeting to me. Which is okay, I guess, but it isn't exactly what I was expecting. It's going to take a little getting used to."

The room was silent.

"That's all," said Bernie.

"Thanks, Bernie," said the room.

I looked around at my friends. "I'm Nate," I said.

"Hi, Nate."

The room reverberated with masculinity. I took a deep breath. "Most of you came to this meeting because I invited you. Some of you have been meeting with me individually for months or years. Some of you have seen me in other meetings or maybe heard me teach in this church. You may be expecting me to teach tonight, but that's not what this group is all about. The Samson Society, as I see it, is not an expert-based organization, and it does not have a single leader or class of leaders. Anybody can lead. Everybody can contribute. We're building this fellowship on the conviction that on any given day every Christian needs help and every Christian has some help to give.

"That being said, I did spend some time today drafting a meeting format that I'd like to submit for our use as we get started. What I've written is not sacred, and it is certainly not perfect. Anybody can write a different meeting format—and I hope someone will—but for now what I've written can at least give us a starting place. Is that okay?" There were murmurs of assent.

I looked at one of my close friends. "Mark, would you lead the meeting?"

Mark shrugged. "Sure, if you want me to."

I said, "I also have four readings here that other guys can do at the appropriate times. Who will volunteer for a reading?" Four men raised their hands, and I passed the selections to them.

Mark glanced down at the typewritten format I'd prepared. "Hi, I'm Mark," he said.

"Hi, Mark," said the room.

"Let's open this meeting with prayer, followed by a reading of the Twenty-third Psalm." We bowed our heads as Mark led us in a simple prayer. When we were finished, Glenn read the Twenty-third Psalm. A reverent quietness settled over the room.

Finally Mark spoke. "Welcome to this meeting of the Samson Society," he read. "We are a company of Christian men. We are also natural *loners,* who have recognized the dangers of isolation and are determined to escape them, natural *wanderers* who are finding spiritual peace and prosperity at home, natural *liars* who are now finding freedom in the truth, natural *judges* who are learning how to judge ourselves aright, and natural *strongmen* who are experiencing God's strength as we admit our weaknesses.

"As Christians, we meet at other times for worship, for teaching, or for corporate prayer. Today, however, we meet to talk. Our purpose is to assist one another in our common journey. We do so by sharing honestly, out of our own personal experience, the challenges and encouragements of daily Christian living in a fallen world.

"Our faith rests in the love of God, as it is revealed in his Word and in the life of his Son. This is the great 'Fact' of the gospel, which is the foundation of our charter. Who has the Fact?"

"I do," said Jonathan, waving the paper I had given him. "This is the Fact."

"Hi, Jonathan," said Bernie, grinning.

"Oops, sorry. I'm Jonathan."

"Hi, Jonathan," said the room.

"This is the Fact. Number one. *God exists*. In the timeless mystery of the Trinity, he is perfectly harmonious, perfectly whole.

"Number two. *God is our Creator*. He designed us to live in eternal harmony with him and each other, and to care for the rest of his creation.

"Three. Spurning God's fellowship, *we all have sinned*, forfeiting our created place and losing our spiritual lives.

"Four. *I have personally defied God's law and rejected his love*. Alienation from him has produced darkness and chaos in my life, for which I have often blamed others.

"Five. *God has continued to love me*, even in my active rebellion, and in Christ has done everything necessary to restore me perfectly to himself.

"Six. As I accept responsibility for my sin and find forgiveness in the finished work of Christ, *I experience reconciliation with God* and am progressively restored to harmony with myself and others.

"And seven. Despite the lingering effects of sin, *I am a restored son of the sovereign Lord*, whose Spirit is at work in my weakness, displaying his glory and advancing his kingdom."

"Thanks, Jonathan," said the room.

Mark took over again. "Let's take a moment to introduce ourselves," he said, reading from the meeting format. "I'll begin and we'll go around the room. Those who wish may give a one-sentence statement of their reason for attending this meeting."

Mark looked up and smiled. "I'm Mark," he said.

"Hi, Mark!"

"I came to this meeting tonight with a lot of curiosity and, to be honest, a little bit of fear, but what I'm feeling right now is mostly hope, a suspicion that something wonderful is going to happen. I'm glad to be here."

"Thanks, Mark!" said the room.

The introductions progressed quickly as each man—Tom, Bruce, Mike, Glenn, Michael, Bernie, Michael, Mark, Jonathan, Mark, Dave, and David—described in condensed form the feelings or circumstances that had drawn him to the meeting.

When the last guy had introduced himself, Mark resumed. "We in the Samson Society have been set upon a Path, a way of living that leads to godliness and freedom. Here is the description of that Path that is given in our charter." He looked around. "Who has the Path?"

"I'm Mike," said Mike.

"Hi, Mike!"

"Here's the Path. Number one. Believing the Fact, I surrender to God in simple faith, making no promises, but merely asking for his aid.

"Two. I start attending meetings of the Society, and from its members I select a *Silas*, a trustworthy traveling companion for this stretch of the road.

"Three. In honest detail I describe to God and to my Silas the course and consequences of my attempts to live apart from God.

"Four. Encouraged by my Silas and others, I develop the daily disciplines of prayer, study, and self-examination. I abandon self-help, asking God instead to do for me what I cannot do for myself.

"Five. I choose to trust the body of Christ, weighing the wisdom of my friends when facing decisions and seeking their strength when confronted by temptation.

"Six. When I can do so without injuring anyone, I make amends for damage I have caused. If direct amends are impossible or inadvisable, I demonstrate my repentance in other ways.

"And number seven. I offer myself as a Silas to others. Each day I ask God for the grace to seek his kingdom rather than my own, to serve those he places in my path rather than serving myself."

"Thanks, Mike," said the room.

Mark said, "Okay, we have now reached the *sharing* portion of our meeting. In sharing, we speak honestly out of our own experience. We tell the truth about ourselves, knowing that our brothers will listen to us in love and will hold whatever we say in strictest confidence. We try to keep our comments brief, taking care to leave plenty of time for others. We address our statements to the group as a whole rather than directing them toward any one person. As a rule, we refrain from giving advice to others or instructing them during the meeting, believing that such conversations are best reserved for private moments between friends.

"The suggested topic today is, let's see—" He looked over the collection of topics listed on the meeting guide and selected one. "Okay, the suggested topic tonight is *fear*, but we are not confined to that subject. You may speak about any issue that is currently commanding your attention. The floor is now open for anyone who wishes to speak."

A silence settled over the room. I looked around, wanting to speak but feeling I should allow someone else to break the ice. A few guys sat with their eyes closed. Others examined their hands or looked at the floor. Finally, Dr. McCurdy spoke up. "I'm Bruce, and I guess I'll go first."

"Hi, Bruce!"

I was eager to see how a professional counselor would handle this delicate situation. Would Bruce speak in general terms, avoiding any personal disclosures? I wouldn't blame him if he did. Would he take an educator's approach, drawing on his years of advanced study and clinical experience to teach us all something useful about anxiety? He was certainly capable of playing the expert if he chose to.

Choosing his words carefully, Bruce said, "Fear is an appropriate topic for me today, because I've been a little fearful about coming to this meeting. I've been wondering whether this really is an appropriate place for me to be transparent. Because I work full time at the church, privacy is a practical consideration for me. There are also ethical issues for me to consider, professional rules that limit my conduct even in nonprofessional settings. So I've been running this debate in my head. One voice says that the safest thing for me to do is just stay in my office, but another voice says that isolation is the riskiest option of all. I am not a rock. I'm not capable of being my own counselor or my own best friend. For me to live a healthy and balanced life, I need to be real around other guys."

Looking at Mike Malloy, the only other therapist in the group, Bruce continued, "I've decided that I will ask another professional counselor to be my Silas, and I'll tell him the really *private* stuff, but I will also come here and participate as a full member of this team. I will not allow the fear of exposure to keep me from taking my place in the human race and participating in the body of Christ."

Bruce continued for a few minutes, speaking frankly about his fears and the steps he was taking to overcome them. When he was finished, another man shared, and then another.

I listened in awe as the conversation unfolded. Each man brought his own story to the table, contributing a few fragmentary personal insights on the subject at hand. Each man led with his weakness, but most guys also had some experience, strength, or hope to share. Some quoted Scripture. The progression of the conversation sparked my own thinking. Eventually I took the floor and found myself saying things I had not expected to say.

The last man to speak was Dave Bunker, a recent transplant from Chicago. Dave is a big guy, and he cannon-balled into the deep end of the topic with a thunderous, magnificent display of brutal honesty. His brief contribution was dazzlingly direct, exquisitely humble, and it resonated with the raw power of simple faith. Dave concluded by saying, "I'm glad to know that there are brothers here in Tennessee that I can say this kind of stuff to. It's an honor to be here. Even though I'm meeting most of you for the first time, I already feel like I can trust you guys."

By the time the sharing ended, I knew that something significant had taken place. God had been present in our conversation. Somehow, despite the absence of a sermon or a formal Bible study, we had all been instructed, exhorted, encouraged, reproved, corrected, and strengthened in our faith. We had experienced real fellowship, and I could already sense a fresh spiritual bond between us.

Five minutes before the end of the hour, Mark asked, "Are there any final thoughts?" No one spoke. "Okay," Mark said, picking up the meeting guide. "The formal part of our meeting is now coming to a close, but you are encouraged to stay around afterward to talk, or to adjourn elsewhere for more informal fellowship. Are there any announcements related to this meeting?"

"I'm Nate," I said.

"Hi, Nate!"

"I'd like to suggest McCreary's Irish Pub on Main Street as a place to hang out after this meeting. A young Christian couple, Darryl and Annie McCreary, own it. My daughter Kristin works there. You don't have to drink alcohol to get a table, and the fish-and-chips are terrific."

"Thanks, Nate."

Mark continued, "As valuable as they are, these meetings are no substitute for daily Christian friendship. Just as our Lord's first disciples were sent into the world two-by-two, we too should look for at least one Christian companion, a fellow traveler and advisor with whom to share this stretch of the road. The person we choose will be flawed and weak as we are, but he will listen to our story, protect our confidence, and talk with us briefly every day. We will walk together by mutual consent, gracefully accepting the fact that relationships change over time and few relationships are permanent. Love, honesty, and humility are our watchwords.

"Before we close, let us reaffirm the Pact under which our Society operates." Mark looked up. "Who has the Pact?"

"I'm Tom," said Tom.

"Hi, Tom!"

"And here's the Pact. One. God is the sole owner of the Samson Society and its only authority. No member may speak for the entire Society.

"Two. All members of the Society are equals—friends and fellow servants, bound by love and honor. No member may command the obedience of another.

"Three. The Society owns no property, collects no dues or fees, pays no salaries, incurs no debts.

"Four. The Society is an extension of the Church Universal. It is not a corporate entity and can make no contracts with congregations, denominations, causes, or campaigns, regardless of their merit.

"Five. Any two or more persons who believe the Fact, who agree to follow this Path and join this Pact, may initiate a meeting of the Samson Society.

"Six. We hold in strictest confidence any personal information shared by other members, unless permission to divulge it is given by any whom its disclosure might affect.

"And seven. Members are fully authorized to create and distribute, freely or for profit, personal explanations and applications of the Society's principles—if they neither alter nor violate its charter and do not prohibit others from copying their work."

"Thanks, Tom!"

Mark said, "Let's stand and close with the Lord's Prayer."

Rising to our feet and joining hands, we recited the prayer that Christians have been relaying to heaven since our Lord first taught it to us. The familiar words now carried new weight for me. "*Our* Father . . . Give *us* this day *our* daily bread. . . . Deliver *us* from evil." I was not an individual standing in a sea of strangers, bawling my private petitions to God, begging *my* father for *my* bread, and asking him to deliver *me*. No, this time my brothers and I were approaching God together as his sons, expressing our devotion to him in unison. A few short minutes of authentic fellowship had created a communion among us, a spiritual bond that deepened our sense of connection with God.

The simplicity and power of that moment gave me chills.

The Meeting After the Meeting

After that first Samson meeting, most of us drove to McCreary's to hang out for a while, inaugurating the "meeting-after-the-meeting" that would quickly become a standard feature of Samson culture. It would also become, in some quarters, the most controversial thing we do. I still get plenty of questions about it today.

"You meet at a *pub?*" an incredulous Christian will ask me.

"*Our* group does, yes. Some other groups go to coffee shops or restaurants after their meetings."

"You go to a *bar*, where they serve *liquor?*"

"No, McCreary's doesn't have a liquor license, but they do serve some wonderful Irish beer—Guinness, Smithwick's, and Harp— along with their fish-and-chips and Irish stew."

"So you *drink?*"

"Some of us will have a pint. Others won't. It really depends on how much a guy likes beer. If he doesn't like it at all, he orders soda or coffee. If, like several guys in Samson, he likes it *too much*, then he's probably already talked about that problem within the safety of the group and he chooses a nonalcoholic drink instead. Either way, it's not a big deal."

"Not a big deal! Isn't drinking contrary to everything you stand for?"

That's when I try to explain that not all Christians view drinking in the same way. Many of the men in our group, for example, are Presbyterians, heirs to a tradition that has always placed a high value on moderation. I point out that John Calvin's annual salary package, when he was pastoring the thriving church in Geneva, included 250 gallons of wine for him and his guests. I mention that Luther's wife, Catherine, was a skilled brewer with her own recipe, a strong beer that the great reformer enjoyed every day he was home. I allude to the little-known fact that after the Pilgrims landed at Plymouth Rock, the first permanent building they erected was a brewery. And I quote C. S. Lewis's famous line from *Mere Christianity:* "It is a mistake to think that Christians ought all to be teetotalers; [Islam], not Christianity, is the teetotal religion."

C. S. Lewis wrote that line for a good reason. He was addressing post-Christian England, trying to convey the essence of the gospel to a culture that had forgotten the faith. Much of the popular resistance to Christianity, Lewis knew, had been provoked by the militant rhetoric of the temperance movement, an experiment in social engineering in which Christians (especially Christian women) had played a prominent role. Even though Prohibition had failed miserably in America, its polarizing effects were still being felt on both sides of the Atlantic, and the church was all mixed up in it. The simplicity of the gospel had been lost in the fervor of the fight over alcohol. Like the legalists that Paul had opposed in first-century Galatia, Christian teetotalers were imposing an extra requirement upon twentieth-century audiences, insisting that every Christian take a vow of abstinence from alcohol. The result? Non-Christians were ignoring or rejecting the message of the church, *and for good reason.*

That's why when people suggest that our Samson group move its meeting-after-the-meeting to a place that doesn't serve alcohol in order to avoid offending Christians who think drinking is a sin, I vote against it. After all, I personally know several men who only attended their first Samson meeting *because* we go to the pub afterward. Our willingness to be real, our determination to give secondary issues secondary status, gave us credibility with these guys. Other Samson groups have decided the matter differently, mostly out of concern for alcoholics within their ranks, and that's perfectly fine too. I know of one group that convenes at a Denny's after the meeting, another that gets together at a Mexican restaurant. The important thing, in my estimation, is not where we meet or what we drink when we get there. The important thing is that we bring our true selves to a place where we can talk honestly about ultimate things, a place where free and easy conversation can build a bridge to authentic fellowship.

The Pirate Monks

On that first night at the pub we made an important decision. We needed a new meeting place. The Women's Parlor was comfortable, but it was the wrong setting for a men's meeting like ours. Beginning the following week, we would gather in an ordinary church classroom and sit on folding chairs.

It was also at the pub, about a year after we started, that our group gained its nickname. By this time, our weekly gathering had grown to about twenty-five guys, and the meeting-after-the-meeting was taking up half the pub. What happened that night was probably inevitable. Eventually, if you cram enough guys into one room and give some of them beer, somebody is going to start talking like a pirate. This is especially true if one of those guys has only one leg. Joe Shore, our one-legged communication czar, fueled the merriment, and soon we were all swinging our mugs and making bawdy nautical references.

Then, suddenly, a latecomer arrived at the pub with a desperate prayer request. News quickly spread through the room. One guy stood up and called for prayer. Immediately we all laid our mugs on the tables, bowed our heads, and prayed. When the prayer was finished, we sat in reverent silence for a few moments, savoring the flavor of the experience.

Scott Dente broke the silence. "I've got it!" he said.

"What?" asked Joe.

"The two words that perfectly describe the Samson Society! *Pirate Monks!*"

"Aaaarrrggghh!" said Joe grinning.

"Aaaarrrggghh!" we all cried, raising our mugs in a raucous salute to the brotherhood of sinner-saints.

◄ Eleven ►

How It Works
A Narrated Tour of the Path

A MAN'S FIRST SAMSON MEETING CAN BE AN OVERWHELMING experience. There are probably a lot of guys in the room he doesn't know, and as the meeting progresses he hears some terminology that doesn't sound familiar. But because the guys say their names every time they speak, he starts learning names right away, and because they read the Society's central principles aloud at every meeting, he soon begins to figure out what the group believes, what it does, and how it goes about doing it.

It doesn't take the newcomer very long to understand that the Samson strategy for living is summarized in the central column of its charter—the Path. The seven stages of the Path are discussed often at Samson meetings and retreats. (In fact, a few guys in Franklin recently spun off a special Saturday discussion meeting, complete with a workbook, to dig deeper into the reasons, routines, and resources for this new way of life.)

Nothing in the Path is new, of course. This is basic Christian discipleship, practical spirituality with a rich heritage firmly rooted in the Bible. Rather than setting forth a devotional method that marginalizes God and individualizes the Christian faith, the Path helps us face the fact that it is always *God* who saves and restores us, and he is saving and restoring us all *together*.

I don't pretend to be the world's expert on the Path. In my view, no one guy can possibly explain it fully. If you really want to learn the Path, I advise you to join a group of men who are actually walking on it. But to give you an introduction, I'll go through the Path stage by stage and explain my perspective on it. Here goes—

Stage One

Believing the Fact, I surrender to God in simple faith, making no promises but merely asking for his aid.

I'm a lousy dancer, and for good reason. I grew up thinking dancing was a sin, or at least a *pre*-sin. Like going to the movies, dancing was one of those worldly activities that real Christians shun because it leads inevitably to sex. My parents—who may have danced quite a bit, given the size of our family—prohibited us from attending any function where dancing might be committed. They even sent a note to the school office each year stipulating that their children were to be excused from square dancing in gym class. In my capacity as class president I helped plan many school dances, but I never attended any of them. On the night of the senior prom, while my classmates were preening in tuxes and gowns, I was quaffing Hi-C punch and exchanging testimonies with gingham-clad Christian girls at the junior-senior banquet in the church fellowship hall. Not that I'm bitter or anything.

Since leaving home I have broken nearly every other childhood taboo with gusto, but I have not yet disentangled myself from the dancing inhibition. No matter how happy or romantic I feel, I just cannot get my body to cooperate. Do I wanna dance? Yes! Can I? Lord knows I've tried. At joyous family occasions like my daughter's wedding and my wife's birthday party, I've taken the woman I love in my arms and swept her absolutely nowhere. The best I can manage is a slowly rotating cheek-to-cheek clinch, performed with acute embarrassment.

My friend Steve, who belongs to a ballroom dancing club, insists that I can learn to dance. He says it's really easy once you learn the basic steps. One two three, one two three, one two three, turn. And thanks to my experience in the Samson Society, I'm almost ready to let Steve teach me.

My recent life journey has taught me that the expanding life of Christian liberty, the ongoing process of emancipation that the Bible calls sanctification, is not a death march to holiness. No, it's a dance—a beautiful and intoxicating dance *that God leads*. For people who are accustomed to marching, the rhythm of the dance feels very awkward at first. Most of us trip and fall a lot in the beginning, but eventually we catch on. The secret of staying on our feet, we learn, is described in the first stage of the Path. It consists of three simple steps. *Believe, surrender, ask*. Repeat. One two three, one two three, one two three, turn.

Believe

The Samson Society charter opens with a seven-point statement of faith we call "the Fact." We read this simple summary of the gospel aloud at every meeting, reminding ourselves of Christianity's bedrock beliefs. *God exists. He created us for a purpose. I deliberately rejected him, but God did not reject me. Christ has brought me back to God. I am now God's restored son, and he is using even my weaknesses to bring his purposes to pass.*

During my years of active addiction, I did not believe the Fact. Even though I grew up singing "Jesus Loves Me" in Sunday school, I did not believe that he loved me unconditionally. Because I did not fathom my own rebellious heart or recognize God's relentless pursuit of it, I constantly begged forgiveness that was already mine, foolishly promising to "pay God back" with a life of pure obedience if he would give me just one more push, one more chance to redeem myself.

For me, the life of moral improvement was exhausting. It's hard work, being your own savior, and I could never finish the job. I wanted to please God, but I kept getting stuck. Even when I did break loose and lurch forward in a spurt of "spiritual progress," I'd invariably wind up, days later, back in the same familiar rut, cursing myself for my stupidity. Would I never get it right?

Superstition and religion tell me that *God responds to me*. God is powerful, to be sure, but *I* am the real center of the universe, because God's actions are predicated upon mine. Religion and superstition say that I can make God dance by being good, and that by being bad I can force him from the floor.

The gospel says something entirely different. The gospel says that God always leads. He is always the initiator, and his actions are always loving. The gospel says that we love because God loved us first.

For those of us in the Samson Society, the "Path that leads to godliness and freedom" begins with faith in an objective Fact. The ability to recognize and believe that Fact comes as a gift from God. It reaches each of us by personal revelation, like a heavenly visitor arriving at the perfect time, and it inevitably produces surrender.

Surrender

In April of 1945, the battered remnants of Germany's vaunted military machine were trapped in Berlin. Their earlier invasion of the Soviet Union had taken more than 3 million Soviet lives before ending in failure, and the bloodiness of that campaign had given the Soviets an insatiable appetite for revenge. Now, as the Third Reich toppled on the brink of collapse, 2.5 million Soviets were advancing against Berlin on three fronts, and they were moving fast. A wave of panic swept through the German capital.

The Nazis knew that the Western Allies, under the command of General Eisenhower, had been moving toward Berlin from the west, but the Americans had halted on the far side of the Elbe. Now, as the encircling Soviets blasted the city with the fiercest artillery bombardment in history, German troops launched a desperate bid to break through the Soviet lines and reach the Americans.

The Germans finally understood that they were finished as a fighting force. Surrender was inevitable. Only one question remained—*to whom would they surrender?* Would they capitulate to the enemy who

hated them and had sworn to exact vengeance, or would they surrender to another power whose ultimate intentions were more benign?
Defeated German soldiers *ran toward the Americans*, submitting to
them with gratitude and unfeigned relief.

Most of us are slow to recognize that we have lost the war against
our besetting sin. We deceive ourselves about the progress of that war,
taking false comfort in inconsequential successes, distracting ourselves with elaborate battle plans and issuing orders to internal forces
we cannot control. Our losses continue to mount, affecting everyone
around us, but we ignore them. We imagine that we are "fighting the
good fight" against sin, but the battle is already lost. All that remains
is the formality of surrender—and the opportunity, the wondrous
alternative, of *surrendering to God instead*.

Until we grasp the magnitude of our defeat, the prospect of surrendering to God is distasteful to us. We recoil at the thought of giving up, fearing a loss of our imagined liberty, and we frantically carry
on our feeble resistance. But on that great and awful day when the
inner defensive ring finally collapses, we fall toward God exhausted,
and there to our inexpressible relief we find welcome instead of
rebuke, dignity instead of shame, and life instead of death.

Ask

I made a lot of trips to the altar in my early life, often while the piano
played "I Surrender All." I always thought I was surrendering, but I
wasn't. I was negotiating.

My time at the rail always ended with a pledge. I'd sing something
like, "I'll go where you want me to go, dear Lord. I'll be what you
want me to be," and I'd mean every word of it. In that moment I
somehow believed that all my previous broken promises to God had
resulted from imperfect understanding or a lack of resolve. But now
the situation had changed. The preacher had shown me the truth,
and God was offering me a second chance. I finally knew what to do,
and I was determined to do it *from now on*. "I'll go where you want
me to go, dear Lord. I'll be what you want me to be."

A Journey of the Heart

God sought me out in the spring of 2000, to a season of deliverance, healing, and counseling. While our men's ministry studied the book *Wild at Heart*, I began to recognize links between masculinity and spirituality for the first time. In the spring of 2001 I traveled to Colorado for a *Wild at Heart* boot camp, during which John Eldredge challenged us to start asking God for brothers when we returned home.

The week in Colorado was a mountaintop experience for me, but when I got home and prayed for a band of brothers, nothing happened. My wife and I were leading a home fellowship group at the time, but those get togethers weren't meeting my need for male companionship. I enjoyed my Sunday school class, but I was still feeling isolated. It was in that class where I first heard Nate speak, and I remember resonating with his heart. I knew, somehow, that he was a marked man, that God was pursuing him, and somehow I knew that God was pursuing me too.

All that would change in 2003. That spring my wife, Pamela, discovered she was pregnant—with twins! The news was awesome, a true double blessing, but it also scared me a little. The doctor put Pamela on bed rest, and my life started unraveling. After dinner each night, Pamela would go to bed and I would clean up and put our son to bed. Then later, after the house settled down, some deep part of my restless heart would begin screaming. I felt alone and neglected, as though dropped on the curb for this season of my life. I wanted attention, affection, companionship, admiration, and other things I couldn't articulate. I'm sorry to say, I rarely reached for my Bible, but found more immediate distractions: food, television, fantasy, and Internet porn.

One night about 2:00 a.m. I turned off the computer and

cried out to God, asking him again for a brother. "Why don't you give Nate Larkin a call?" an inner voice prompted. That startled me, because I didn't really know Nate, but next day I called him and we met at Starbucks.

On this cold and rainy day in December, 2003, we took our seats at a corner table, and I began to open up a bit about my struggles. Nate sat with me and listened, looking me straight in the eye. As I grew more uncomfortable, he finally invited me to go for a walk, and in that next hour my life changed.

Nate shared his brokenness with me in an open way that stunned my cynical heart. I felt rescued; I found the brother I had been praying for. Later that day, we attended his twelve-step meeting, where Nate introduced me to more guys who were open about their struggles.

Soon Nate, Tom Jackson and I were dreaming together about a place where Christian men could speak honestly about their struggles and strengths, a place where faith and recovery would go hand-in-hand, where guys could say things out loud for the first time, and where a man's worth and dignity would be based on the gospel alone. That dream came to life a month after my twins were born.

More than two years later, God has put together my band of brothers. They are real live men who know the whole me. They tell me that I am a man, and they remind me that I have more value than I realize. They continually remind me of my strength in Christ. Their love has changed me. It has made me a better man. Ask my wife, my kids, my friends—they'll tell you. I'm not perfect, but I am known and loved well by these men.

When I go to Samson meetings and look around the room, I see real men, brave men who struggle out loud with their addictions and failures, and who share their experience and success with humility. By God's grace, we are all experiencing Christ's strength as we admit our weaknesses.

Glenn McClure

I have found that for short stretches of time I can convince myself that I am being faithful to God if I define faithfulness in terms of only one behavior. If I decide that holiness consists of not drinking, for example, I can feel pretty good about myself as long as I don't drink. Even though I treat drinkers with contempt and sin against love in a thousand other ways, I can swagger through the streets and parade into the temple with my head held high, noisily thanking God that "I am not like other men."

Self-righteousness, however, is a double-edged sword. If I have reduced holiness to a single behavior, then I am standing on one leg. One slip and I am nothing again, absolutely useless. Either way, the commandments of the gospel mean nothing to me. I do not hear "Love your wife" or "Love your enemies" or "Love your neighbors as you love yourself." I only hear "Don't drink."

God, in his grace, has used addiction to shatter my moralistic understanding of the Christian faith and force me to accept the gospel. I am not a faithful man. That's why I need a Savior. I cannot live victoriously on my own. That's why I need a Helper and brothers. I cannot keep my promises to God—the very act of making them is delusional—but God will keep his promises to me.

As a Christian, I am perpetually reduced to the role of a supplicant. No more can I offer God a bargain, his favor in exchange for my faithfulness, or go toe-to-toe with him, *demanding* payment for years of service. But when I approach him humbly, as a restored prodigal son, he responds with overwhelming generosity to my requests for aid.

No fancy prayers are required. In fact, God finds fancy prayers repugnant. He loves it, however, when I acknowledge my need and my belief in his benevolence with a simple one-word prayer:

"*Help!*"

Stage Two

I start attending meetings of the Society, and from its members I select a *Silas*, a trustworthy traveling companion for this stretch of the road.

During my adolescent years I sometimes dreamed of running away from home. I made a plan. I would slip out of my window one night, retrieve my backpack from the barn, and then hike cross-country, avoiding towns, until I reached the hills. I would search the hills until I found a cave that I could make my home. The cave would be perfect. From its mouth I would be able look out over the faraway farms and the road that wound through the valley. I would see anyone who approached me, but no one would be able to see me. In my cave, I would be safe.

I never did run away from home, but I managed to find the cave anyway. It was right inside my own head. I made that private place my fortress, my sanctuary. In my cave, I felt safe.

Here's the thing about caves: they feel much safer than they really are. Sure, you can hide in a cave, but if your enemy discovers where you are hiding, he can trap you there. And there's always the risk of a cave-in.

Also, a cave is not really very comfortable. You can cushion the floor with carpets and paint pictures on the walls, but it's still dark inside a cave, and the temperature is always about fifty-five degrees. If you want to get warm, you have to burn something.

And a cave dweller doesn't really go anywhere. He may watch the traffic passing on the road below. At night he may catch voices of travelers as they sit around their campfires discussing the world beyond the valley. But he won't join them, because that would mean leaving the safety of the cave.

I lived in my cave until I was forty-two years old. By that time, my sanctuary had become a prison. I felt trapped. I was hungry, I was cold, and I was almost out of fuel. Nearly everything I had ever owned had gone into the fire, and now it was dark again.

In the Gospels, Jesus sometimes encountered guys like me. The crazy Gadarene, for example, who lived in the caves on the far side of the Sea of Galilee (see Mark 5). Jesus restored that man to his right mind and sent him into town. And don't forget Lazarus, entombed four days in a cave outside of Bethany. Jesus wept outside of that cave. Then he said, "Lazarus, come out of there!" (see John 11:43).

To follow the Path, you must first leave the cave.

Bringing the Full Weight

I stepped out of the pub after sharing a pint and some jovial conversation with some men I have grown to love and respect over the last year. I have chosen to sit in a room on Monday nights with guys who are trying to figure it out—not so much the meaning of life, the keys to success, or the pathways to happiness, but simply how to be present in their own lives rather than merely existing while life swirls around them. These guys are deeply engaged in a dialog born out of weakness, and I have been surprised by how much I love them. We are a group of sinners, addicts, haters, drinkers, smokers, liars, and thieves. We are all at least one of these things. We are also followers of Christ. Every week we come together to share the journey. We speak the language of brokenness, the language of commitments severed, of confidences lost, relationships destroyed, and mostly, the language of restoration and recovery.

After our meetings we step over to the Irish pub and let our souls and stomachs grow warm. This night I decided to walk across the street to a movie theater. The air was crisp and I could see my breath.

My head was still spinning from a conversation in the pub about the gospel story and how we tell it. When we find the gospel to be true and we begin to wrestle with its implications, we are eventually forced to face our stubborn humanity and admit that we are still the walking wounded, broken yet perpetually healing. But there's a problem—contemporary church culture requires us to give the appearance of victory. There are subjects that church people cannot talk about. There are activities that church people do not engage in. There are places we do not hang out, girls we do not call, hotel rooms where things do not happen, computers that do not show images that are destructive, relationships that are not failing, abuses that are not stealing joy. In church, there is no shadow or darkness to speak of.

In church we are allowed to speak of past victories over sin, but not battles that are still underway. As a result we promote a gospel of our own construction. This is not the gospel the New Testament talks about, the foundation strong enough to bear the weight of the world and the depravity of the redeemed. Ours is flimsy, too fragile to carry our failures.

On Monday nights and throughout the week, my friends and I challenge each other with this mandate: "Bring the full weight of who you are into your relationships." When we "show up" fully in our relationships, we give others the chance to know us, and we give them permission to be known.

Every man has something in his life that makes him unique— some brokenness that sets him apart from those around him. Though we have similarities to one another, our differences lie in the way joy enters into our secrets, the way light exposes our darkness. Ultimately it is our redemption that looks unique. It is the way healing comes, how long it takes, and who is involved that displays the endless creativity of God.

Our church culture and our Christian music community have not given us permission to be ourselves and bring the full weight of who we are into our musical conversations, our movies, our pulpits, or our youth group halls...and watching this, I have decided that perhaps, after all, it is best to keep the weight on.

Dan Haseltine
(Adapted, with permission, from an article that first appeared in *Relevant* magazine.)

Meetings

For many of us in the Samson Society, that first step was absolutely terrifying. It's hard to leave the safety of your dorm or office or house, drive to a new place, and walk into an unfamiliar room filled with strangers. It's harder still to venture outside the cave in your head, to join the circle around the fire, to sit where other people can see you, and say things out loud that are true and dangerous.

A Silas

But even joining the circle is not enough. The Samson Society does not consist merely of meetings. Joining a circle once a week to speak the truth about yourself will give you a *taste* of fellowship, but it is not the level of fellowship that will take you somewhere new, somewhere outside of the valley. To experience that level of change, you must get up the next morning and join this band of travelers on the road. You must fall in step with one of them and walk beside him for a while, talking about whatever comes up. We call that traveling companion a *Silas*, a name that comes from the Bible.

In the early church, Christians almost always traveled in groups or in pairs, following the example and admonition of Jesus. Paul, the first missionary to the Western world, traveled for three years with a man named Barnabas. A few years later, Paul and Barnabas decided to make a second trip. But a problem came up; they couldn't agree on the details. Eventually they split up, and Barnabas sailed off with somebody else.

What would Paul do now? Would he go on alone? He was *the apostle Paul* after all, a bona fide spiritual superstar, a soloist who didn't need a band. But Paul knew better. At the next meeting of the local church, he looked around the room and picked out a guy, a humble and wise and trustworthy guy named Silas, and he asked that guy to travel with him. Silas agreed, and within days they were on their way.

In the Samson Society, we say that everybody needs a Silas and everybody should eventually *become* a Silas. The Silas relationship is not assigned by anyone; you pick a guy you trust. If he agrees, you make an open-ended arrangement to walk together for this stretch of the road, however long it lasts. Your relationship may end after just a few weeks—in fact, some guys will offer to be your *temporary Silas*, just to get you started. Or it may last for many months or years. At every step along the way, both guys are free to alter the arrangement for any reason—no questions asked and no hard feelings. Few Silas relationships are permanent. They last as long as they *need* to last, and they end graciously.

But in the meantime, both of you must take this Silas thing seriously. Your Silas will usually ask you to call him every day and talk for a few minutes about what you're feeling, what you're doing, and what you're planning to do. He'll listen, and he'll offer encouragement and feedback. He will also probably ask you to sit down with him sometime for an extended visit and tell him your story. Knowing your story will help your Silas place your struggles in context, make connections you might not notice on your own, and remember things you'd rather forget. Wherever you are on the Path, he'll press you to do the work appropriate to that stage and then move on to the next one.

Some guys put off enlisting a Silas because they're still looking for the all-wise, all-knowing, all-caring guy. That guy doesn't exist. A good Silas will be just as flawed and weak as you are, but he will possess one priceless quality—*he won't be you!* As a compassionate outsider, he'll be able to look at your life objectively and help you understand exactly where you are.

Some guys enlist a Silas but then don't call him, usually because they don't want to impose. What they fail to understand is that it's actually your Silas who gains the greatest benefit when you call. Helping others helps a Silas, and challenging others challenges him. Every call he receives is a gift. In fact, the blessings of serving as a Silas are so great that a new Silas may fall prey to the illusion that he can thrive just by taking calls, without making a daily call himself. It's an illusion that produces a debilitating condition we call "Silasitis," with symptoms of pomposity and delusions of grandeur. Fortunately, Silasitis is cured by failure.

And everybody fails. That's what we learn. My friend John Scudder, a former loner who is no stranger to success or failure, recently sent me this description of his closest friends, the men in the Samson Society meeting he attends every week:

I see . . .
a man who is a cancer survivor,
a man whose wife has MS,
a man who is engaged to be married,
a man who is finalizing his divorce,
a man who works too hard,
a man who lives for his family,
a man whose best friend betrayed him,
a man who has five stepchildren,
a man who has been divorced two times,
a man who had three affairs,
a man who struggles with homosexuality,
a man who was sexually abused as a child,
a man who does not know his father,
a man who knows how to fight,
a man who has lost his heart and purpose,
a man who is an alcoholic,
a man who needs no one,
a man who views pornography at work,
a man who lost a million dollars,
a man who has a million dollars,
a man who is struggling as a musician,
a man who is a successful musician,
a man who has a master's degree in divinity,
a man who had open-heart surgery,
a man who is still married even though he had an affair,
a man who is a pastor,
a man who has visited prostitutes,

a man whose child has died,
a man who received a liver transplant,
a man who is a medical doctor.
I see . . . a man.

In the Samson Society, it's our failures even more than our successes that bind our fellowship together. No longer are we spending our days alone in the darkness of our caves, hiding our failures for fear of rejection and ridicule. Instead we are walking together on a sunlit path that is taking us somewhere. We are carrying each other's burdens, and Christ is walking with us. In our experience, the words of the apostle John ring true:

> If we walk in the light as He is in the light, we have fellowship with one another, and the blood of Jesus Christ His Son cleanses us from all sin. (1 John 1:7 NKJV)

Stage Three

**In honest detail, I describe to God and to my Silas
the course and consequences
of my attempts to live apart from God.**

In this section of the Path I'll change the metaphor, describing my life as a sea voyage rather than a journey by land. This stage consists of a long look back—not for purposes of self-justification or self-pity, but for sober self-assessment.

If I am going to alter the direction of my life in any permanent way, I must first acknowledge that I did not arrive at my present position as a pawn of fate or the helpless victim of malevolent forces. It is true, of course, that great powers are at work in the world, and I have certainly encountered many circumstances beyond my control. My tiny ship has always struggled against tides, currents, winds, waves, and even occasional hurricanes. In all that time, however, *I have been at the helm of my ship*, anticipating and responding, acting or failing to act. I have charted and recharted my own course, patching my vessel after every storm and setting my sails with little regard to ultimate reality. Now, finally, the time has come for me to reconstruct that long voyage and calculate the cost of it.

In this stage, I learn to tell my story in a new way. I have always been a storyteller. For as long as I can remember, I have comforted myself and entertained others with tales from my life. Like television-movies-of-the-week, most of my stories have been "fictionalized accounts of actual events," potboilers in which I appear as the fearless adventurer, the unappreciated genius, the jilted lover, or the tragic hero. I enjoy these stories immensely and I desperately want to believe that they are true, but they are not. Not really. And when I attempt to live my life as though they *are* true, their distortions prove destructive.

Now is the time to set the record straight. I begin by taking my bearings. Where am I *now?* This is not an easy question to answer, and I have been answering it poorly for years. My habit has been to make snap judgments, to declare that "I am in a good place" or that "I am in an awful place," and then to focus only on the features of the place that make it good or awful. But the truth is more complex and wonderful. I am in a place. There are elements of this place that are good, and there are other elements that God has promised to *use* for good even though they are awful. And I am not alone. Whether I have fled to the uttermost parts of the sea or made my bed in hell, God has followed me there.

Now I find myself on the shoals of an island, and not for the first time. In fact as I look around, I notice features that are strikingly familiar. I begin to wonder whether I might have found this place on purpose. I am tempted to think that I was drawn here by blind instinct, like the salmon or the swan, but my better judgment tells me that some volition was involved. However it happened, it is clear that my behavior has followed a pattern, and I now set myself to the task of bringing that pattern into focus.

Mapping the Course of My Life

At this point my Silas will probably suggest that I acquire pen and paper—simple tools essential to good chart making—and start mapping the course of my life. He may recommend that I divide my life into five-year blocks and examine each block in detail, noting key events and describing my responses to them.

The first part of that assignment will be fairly easy. I do remember much of what happened to me—especially the damage I sustained from the words and actions of others. Now, however, I focus upon *my* role in the drama, the things I did before and after every engagement, the treasures I buried and the vows I made. My Silas may assist me in this work by probing at the seams of my narrative with pointed questions. What did you feel? Where had you felt that before? What did you do about it? Why?

As it turns out, my journey was not as erratic as it seemed. I spent many years at sea, it is true, but not as a wanderer. Somewhere along the line I discovered a trading route, and I followed that route over and over again. As I reconstruct the list of ports visited and trades made, I see that my black-market enterprise was never really profitable. Its payoffs were poor, and its costs astronomical.

Now my Silas urges me to add up the costs. Some of them I can calculate in financial terms—money I spent on "getting drunk" with my drug of choice, money I wasted while under the influence of my drug, money stolen from me while I was intoxicated, money I paid in penalties for drunken behavior. I can even roughly approximate the financial value of opportunities I lost during binges and the hangovers that followed them.

But there have been other expenses too, costs equally real but harder to quantify. In this long-running business of mine I have paid heavily with my health, my spirituality, my creativity, my peace of mind, and the quality of my relationships. At the mention of relationships the list suddenly grows longer, for I recognize that others have paid dearly for my decisions. I have passed along substantial costs to

Odd Man Out

I am an introvert. I love times of solitude to recharge my batteries, drained by necessary human interaction. Even though I love my family, I like my alone time. But the aloneness allows me space for my sin. The very aloneness that feeds me when I'm at my best, feeds *on* me at my worst. When aloneness takes on the character of isolation, I get in trouble. I seek joy, excitement, salve, and rest from sources not ordained by God, and no one but God knows what I'm doing, because I'm alone.

When I took advantage of a free counseling session at a Christian conference, it was because my isolation and its consequences had gotten out of hand. The counselor strongly encouraged me to give Nate a call. She said something like, "I'll know how serious you are about getting help if you make this phone call."

At my first Samson meeting, I felt a familiar sensation. It's that odd-man-out feeling. I was the only African-American in the group. I lived in Nashville, while most of these guys lived "outside of Nashville." Many of them attended the same church. They were Reformed; I work for the Methodists. It was clear to me that most of these guys knew each other. In those first moments, I felt out of place. I wondered what to expect.

Fortunately that very day I had a long talk with Nate. We shared the basics of our stories. I decided to show up at the meeting because of Nate. It took only fifty minutes for me to see that all those external differences were not important at all. As guys shared their individual stories, I recognized myself. And I felt less alone—in a good way.

I heard men who want to live Christian lives talk honestly about their struggles as men. I heard guys who have sensed, like me, that being a Christian man is neither about being womanly—

as many of our churches imply—nor about being stereotypically macho. Men have feelings, but we tend to express them differently than women do. I heard honest guys talk about their fears, their disappointments, and their sin. And I heard support and identification. I heard myself. I still do.

In time, the meaning of the Samson Society has changed for me. I started attending the group in order to deal with sin. I wish I could say my struggle is all over. More accurately I now have hope that God will, by grace, deal with it and that God will love me regardless of my sin. I'd known this fact intellectually. Through the Samson Society I have experienced that grace and love. And Samson guys have helped me to recognize that grace in other areas of my life. I continue to experience grace through my wife, my children, and my grandson.

The greatest gift of the Samson Society is the recovery of my dreams as they fit with the mission of God. As I have had the opportunity to tell my own story, I have recaptured my dream of being the man I have wanted to be, the man I believe I was created to be. With the vision comes the hard work of looking at those things that get in the way.

I love the words we rehearse at Samson meetings: *We are natural wanderers, liars, judges, and strongmen.* I identify with all of them, but the best wisdom for me in the Samson Society has been identifying that I am a natural-born loner, who has recognized the dangers of isolation and is determined to escape them.

Tony Peterson

parents, siblings, partners, children, friends, employers, colleagues, customers, and even perfect strangers.

Confessing in Honest Detail

Adding up all these costs can be very depressing. As the nature of my scheme becomes apparent, I may feel a strong urge to punish myself. But my Silas intervenes, reminding me that I am a Christian. The punishment for all my sins, he says, has already fallen upon the innocent Savior. Christ does not condemn me, and I must not condemn myself. I will in due time make some amends to others for damage I have caused, but I will never be able to pay for my sins. All that God requires me to do—all that I *can* do—is confess my sins to him in honest detail, accept the mercy he freely extends, and relinquish the rudder of my life to him.

Stage Four

**Encouraged by my Silas and others, I develop
the daily disciplines of prayer, study, and self-examination.
I abandon self-help,
asking God instead to do for me
what I cannot do for myself.**

Looking back, most of us can see that we wrecked our lives in very methodical ways. We were disciplined in our demolition, overcoming advantage and sidestepping success with a rigorous daily regimen of self-destructive behavior. We fed our compulsions faithfully, even while starving our souls, and we seldom missed an appointment with self-hatred. Now, however, the time has come for us to turn our determination in a different direction, to develop disciplines that actually benefit us.

This is not a mere exercise in self-help, nor is it something we can do on our own. In the past, many of us acquired large collections of self-help books, encouraged by the marginal improvement those books produced to imagine that *if we could just find the right information*, we could conquer all our demons and create fundamental change without involving anyone else. For us the real goal of self-improvement was self-sufficiency. Now, however, we recognize that human self-sufficiency is an illusion and self-help is a blind alley. God designed us for collaborative living. As we abandon self-help and devote ourselves instead to loving God and others, the help we need arrives providentially.

Develop Daily Disciplines

Our new friends and our Silas encourage us to replace our old self-destructive routines with the daily disciplines of prayer, study, and self-examination. These changes are not easy to make, for by now our old ways of thinking and acting have become habituated, as automatic as driving to work. We tend to fall into our old patterns without thinking, and we are constantly finding ourselves at familiar destinations without knowing quite how we got there. Patiently and gently, our Silas points out our patterns and offers suggestions for new and better ways of doing things.

For example, when I told my Silas that I was having difficulty starting my day on the right foot, he suggested beginning my day in the evening, like the Jewish Sabbath. He advised me to take some time each night to review the lessons of the previous twenty-four hours and prepare for the morning ahead, doing practical things like setting out the tools and clothes necessary for a good start. "Go to bed early," he said. He counseled me to approach bedtime with gratitude, surrendering my cares to God in prayer and asking him, just before slipping into sleep, to meet me in the morning. Then, upon awakening, I should resume my conversation with God, thanking him immediately for the morning's new mercies and asking him for a continued sense of his presence as I set out on my new routine.

That routine, my Silas said, should include some time devoted to study. "You don't need to spend hours at it," he said. "Even a few minutes of concentrated attention will be beneficial." He advised me to read a short passage of Scripture each day and meditate on it for a

I Was Trapped...

I was trapped, trapped in a prison of my own making. What had started out as simple curiosity had rapidly become, through isolation, pride, and ironically my sense of godly justice, a stronghold from which I could not escape. Life had become meaningless for me, its outcome a foregone conclusion. And I was only twenty-nine.

In my mind, God kept my score in two columns—a plus column and a minus column. For most of my life I'd piled up credits in the plus column, or so I imagined. I attended church, youth group, and church camps. I kept my swearing to a minimum, tried to keep my hormones in check, attended a prestigious Christian college, labored to memorize Bible verses, tried my hand at evangelism, sought out men's groups at the local and national level—all in an effort to stay on God's good side. It seemed to work. The wrongs I committed and the ensuing guilt I felt were fairly rapidly whitewashed with good deeds or excused by good intentions. I was fairly sure God would give me the benefit of the doubt.

But somewhere along the line things started sliding, then cascading, then avalanching into the minus column. My sin— my personal, secret, very unique (I thought) sin swept me to a place of utter shame and unbelief. Before I knew it I was completely out of control. No amount of good works could save me from the dark places where my heart had carried me, and I could never repent enough. I couldn't find a means of escape in any book, conference, tape, or sermon I knew of. Traditional accountability relationships failed to free me. Speaking with pastors and reading the books they recommended didn't help either. For seven years I languished in my prison, trying every escape technique I had been taught in church, but to no avail.

In utter desperation I finally let my secret trickle out to my family and ultimately to a group of men who became the Samson Society. Honesty came hard for me, humility even harder, but as we talked I discovered in the lives of these men amazing parallels to my own story. It was as if we had all been walking through life together, blindfolded. Now we were standing together, blinking in the light of grace, ecstatic to be free of the burden of our secrets. And today we are traveling together, actually going somewhere.

Strange as it may sound, I am tempted to return to solitary confinement every day. But now I have an option. I can pick up the phone and connect with my traveling companions. These are the men who dare to be honest, who are courageous enough to speak openly from their personal experience and give me permission to do the same. In their company I have cried, screamed, shouted, ached, and laughed until I couldn't breathe. These men have helped me taste the full spectrum of human experience. They have made me a better man, a better husband, a better father.

They have also made me a better doctor. In medical school I was taught to examine bodies and diagnose diseases, but in the Samson Society I have learned to sit with people and listen to their stories. I have learned that it is often in our stories that the roots of our diseases can be found. The Samson Society has taught me to see every one of my patients as a person with a story. Every person who comes into my office, no matter how wounded, is a fellow human being, a unique and priceless individual worthy of dignity and honesty and hope. And if I'll listen to the story, I just might hear something that no stethoscope or X-ray would ever reveal.

S.A.R.

little while. He also gave me a list of recommended books that contain practical wisdom for the heart and mind, and suggested reading a page or two each day. It would be helpful, he said, to keep my notebook handy and record the insights that arose during my study time.

My Silas also said that I should use my notebook as a tool for daily self-examination. He suggested opening this time with a simple prayer that David prayed: "Search me, God, and know my heart; test me and know my concerns. See if there is any offensive way in me; lead me in the everlasting way" (Ps. 139:23–24). Then, he said, I should pour out on paper the contents of my heart, writing honestly and fearlessly, secure in the knowledge that nothing—no matter how ugly—can separate me from the love of God.

Abandon Self-Help

Finally, my Silas suggested that I keep a written inventory of my strengths and weaknesses, updating it regularly. In making this inventory I should pay equal attention to both sides of the ledger, neither minimizing my gifts nor exaggerating my defects, and I should ask my friends and family to check its accuracy. He emphasized that since I belong to God, my entire inventory is God's property, and he is capable of using even my weaknesses for good. I should therefore entrust the entire balance sheet to my heavenly Father, allowing him to improve me at the level of my heart rather than disguising my defects with outwardly "good" behavior.

At first blush, these practical suggestions sounded like an awful lot of work. I lodged a diplomatic protest with my Silas, reminding him that I am a busy guy with plenty of responsibilities. With equal diplomacy he reminded me that my self-destructive behaviors had consumed vast amounts of my time for years. He was merely proposing that I substitute a healthy routine for an unhealthy one. He said that if I followed his recommendations, I would probably find myself with much more discretionary time than before, and with more energy and creativity too. His prediction proved astonishingly accurate. I now actually have time to write a book.

Stage Five

**I learn to trust the body of Christ,
weighing the wisdom of my friends when making decisions
and seeking their strength when confronted by temptation.**

I really didn't have close friends in high school, but I hung out sometimes with a guy named Whitmore. Since Whitmore was the biggest
kid in our class and I was the smallest, we made an odd pair.

Naturally, Whitmore played center on the high school basketball
team. I loved basketball and would have given anything for a spot on
the team, but my diminutive stature, along with the absence of any
discernible athletic ability, made that dream unattainable. I managed
to secure a seat on the team bus anyway by volunteering to work as
an equipment manager and statistician.

During school hours Whitmore and I were assigned to several of
the same classes, including a daily study hall. Since neither of us
believed in agonizing over homework, study hall was pretty much a
waste of our time, and we eventually figured out a way to skip it altogether. One day Whitmore filched a pad of passes from the librarian's
desk. Every day thereafter, I'd scrawl a pass for each of us and forge a
teacher's signature on it. Then while the coach was busy teaching a
class in another part of the building, Whitmore and I would go to the
gymnasium, where we would spend the entire period playing one-on-
one basketball.

I suppose that Whitmore and I must have played hundreds of basketball games, maybe thousands. Of that number I won . . . none.
Sometimes Whitmore would stand back and let me shoot, and occasionally he even allowed the score to get close, but when the game
was over it was always Whitmore who had twenty-one points.

Years later I finally got my revenge. By this time I was a father, and
my son Daniel wanted to try out for his school's fifth-grade basketball team. He asked me to teach him how to play. I took Daniel to a
city park near our house, drilled him for a while in the fundamentals,
and then challenged him to a game of one-on-one.

A good father would have let his son win—at least once—but I was too busy being Whitmore to think about that. Time after time Daniel and I returned to the park to play basketball, and game after game I was the one who finished with twenty-one points.

One day, however, Daniel brought a friend along, another ten-year-old who innocently asked if I would play against both of them. I agreed, of course, and whipped them handily. After that first game, however, this kid took Daniel aside for a brief strategy session. When the second game started, I knew I was in trouble.

Daniel's diabolical little friend had a couple of tricks up his sleeve that proved fatal to my game. First, he knew how to "spread the court," so that I couldn't guard both boys at once. Second, he knew how to pass the ball to the open man. With those two tools, the boys quickly wore me out. When the game was over, they had twenty-one points and I was exhausted.

Most of the guys who come into the Samson Society have been playing one-on-one against a superior opponent for years. Sometimes they get the feeling that they are actually going to win, but every game ends the same way. These guys arrive at Samson humiliated and exhausted, hoping we can teach them how to play a better game of one-on-one.

But we don't play that game. We've stopped going one-on-one against a foe who has been matching wits with guys like us for millennia. As far as we know, only one man in history has ever beaten him. ("Immediately the Spirit drove [Jesus] into the wilderness. He was in the wilderness 40 days, being tempted by Satan" (Mark 1:12–13). Every time we've allowed ourselves to be coaxed into a game of one-on-one, we've wound up on the short end of the score. Now we play team ball.

Trust the Body of Christ

To be sure, we have all tried to enlist Jesus in our private contests, and at times we have all felt the empowerment of the Holy Spirit in the fight against temptation. But maintaining the fight on a purely spiritual level has proven impossible for us, and our greatest victories have often been followed by even greater defeats. Now, however, our view of ourselves is more realistic, and our view of Christ has expanded. We finally understand that our bodies—formed of flesh and bone—continually betray us, but *Christ helps us by taking incarnational form in the church*, the motley collection of fellow failures that the Bible insists on calling the *body of Christ.* "Confess your sins to one another," the apostle James urged us, "and pray for one another, so that you may be healed" (James 5:16). We trust Christ by trusting the body of Christ.

When I am facing a difficult decision or a raging temptation, I can demonstrate my faith in Christ by reaching for the telephone and calling a fellow Christian for help. This is not an easy habit to acquire. Every proud and shame-bound instinct in my heart rebels against it. But I do learn to talk with my Silas on a daily basis, and eventually I start calling other guys too, especially the "team" of advisors made up of the guys I know best.

This concept of personal team building is vital to a proper understanding of the Samson Society. Most organizations have an "inner circle," a core group of highly committed people who make all the key decisions for the organization and do most of the work. In these groups, motivated newcomers usually try to find a way into the inner circle and, if that fails, complain about its exclusivity. In the Samson Society, however, we recognize and accept the fact that each man can only sustain a few close relationships. Jesus chose only twelve disciples, and he spent most of his time with just three of them. So we urge every member of our fellowship to build *his own inner circle.* When he moves from Stage Five to Stage Six on the Path, each man should have a team of guys he relies on—guys he knows well, trusts completely, and communicates with on a regular basis.

These teams overlap, since everyone is eligible to play on multiple teams, and the boundaries between them are flexible. They demonstrate our deliberate rejection of centralization. We encourage the formation of small teams while insisting that no team is superior to any other.

Samson Comes to Florida

I'm helping launch a new Samson chapter here in the panhandle of Florida. In fact, last night we held our first meeting at my buddy's office.

After an agonizing thirty-year struggle with the same old sin patterns—addictions to power, money, career, myself, sex, brief relationships, various substances, and material toys—I have found an alternative to the endless downward-spiraling solo cycles of victory and defeat. I've tasted the power of authentic Christian fellowship.

When a friend told me about the Samson Society, I drove to a meeting in Tennessee where I was immediately struck by the open disclosure of stuff I'd never heard mentioned before in a church setting. I thought, *If men can be this ridiculously honest and vulnerable with each other, something dramatic must be happening.*

At Nate's invitation, I joined two dozen Nashville members on a mission trip to San Luis Obispo, California, where they presented the Samson concept to churches in the area. As I watched Christian guys on the central California coast respond to the invitation to start their own community, I was inspired to do the same.

I was beginning to see the absolute necessity of sharing our lives, *including our struggles*, with a community. What a novel concept! I had been trying to live the Christian life in isolation—even though the gospel focuses on community. My lone fight was understandable. After all, most churches are unsafe places to be honest. Nearly everybody maintains a careful façade in a church, and if you dare admit you're a work-in-progress, you run the risk of being branded "unclean" and treated like an outcast.

After tasting the sweet waters of honesty and communion in the Samson fellowships of Tennessee and California, I have a similar vision for my hometown. I am so indescribably hungry for this group that I'm already praying for my future Samson brothers in this area. Though still unknown to me, I am praying for their hearts, their relationships, and the defeats that will lead them to surrender and victory. I am praying that God will reveal these guys to me soon, because even though they don't know it yet, they need me too.

Bill Puryear 111
Destin, FL

But I'm getting ahead of myself. We'll talk more about team dynamics and the value of the individual later in this book, during our discussion of the Pact.

Stage Six

When I can do so without injuring anyone,
I make amends for damage I have caused.
When such amends are impossible or inadvisable,
I demonstrate my repentance in other ways.

One of the most difficult realities for me to accept is the fact that I can never undo all the damage I have done. Even though my life turned around years ago, the people I love still carry scars from wounds I inflicted. Those scars are fading—some are even becoming beautiful in their own way—but their enduring presence will never allow me to forget completely the pain I have caused. I am learning to carry those memories humbly, without complaint or self-loathing.

In the first days after my surrender, when the whole world seemed suddenly alive and I was intoxicated with a new sense of personal freedom, I felt the impulsive urge to sit down with Allie and tell her everything. I naively imagined that a torrent of confession and a round of heartfelt apologies would fix it all. My religious background pushed me in this direction, telling me that I owed my wife an immediate and full disclosure of my past behavior, in all its seamy detail. As daunting as the prospect sounded, the idea of finally unburdening my conscience sounded very appealing to me. I almost did so in an attempt to purchase my own peace of mind.

Living Amends

My new friends stopped me. They assured me that rigorous honesty is essential to recovery and that I should disclose all my sin to someone right away. They said, however, that surprising my unsuspecting wife with a premature confession, broadsiding her with all the lurid details of my betrayal, could cause her grievous mental anguish and do grave emotional harm. I could overwhelm the person I wanted to heal, sweeping her into despair and devastating our relationship beyond all hope of repair. They advised caution in the matter of making amends.

In making amends to my wife, I followed the advice of my twelve-step friends. I began by making a full confession to God on paper, sparing nothing, and then reading that confession aloud to my sponsor. This was not an easy task, but I knew that I could not carry the weight of my secrets any longer, and speaking them out loud helped take their power away.

Following the advice of my new friends, I told Allie that I had changed direction, that I had acknowledged my powerlessness over lust, and was getting help from a group of recovering addicts. I gave her some description of my former behavior, but by employing broad categorical terms I avoided subjecting her to specifics she was unprepared to hear. I told her that from this point forward I was committed to telling the truth—not burdening her with the *whole* truth if she did not request it, but always giving a direct and honest answer to a direct question. This allowed Allie to ask questions when she was emotionally prepared to receive the truth, whatever it was.

I also did my best to relieve my wife of any perceived responsibility for fixing me or monitoring my behavior, explaining that I would now be leaning on my friends for accountability. I let her know that this new way of life would require some time from me each week— time to attend meetings, time to make and receive phone calls, and time for daily spiritual work. Setting aside this time, I explained, would allow me to become much more present at home.

Then, with the encouragement of my friends, I set about making a *living amends* to Allie. Rather than issuing a one-time verbal apology and moving on, I began demonstrating day-by-day that my heart had changed direction. I began accepting criticism rather than reacting to it, embracing responsibility rather than evading it. Slowly and unsteadily I moved from criticizing Allie to encouraging her, from a

. . . A Therapist's Story. . .

I am a man truly blessed. I'm married to a remarkable woman who has loved me in spite of myself for thirty-five years, and I'm a grandpa two times over. I am also an addict in recovery, learning to care for others and myself in better ways. Verbally and emotionally abused as a kid and sexually molested at eleven, I reached adulthood minimizing my childhood history, able to disassociate from the worst of it. As a counselor, I could ignore my stuff by helping others. Not until a recent Samson Society meeting was I able to say for the first time, "I like myself."

I have been a therapist for more than twenty-five years. Much of my weekly caseload consists of men dealing with midlife depression, sexual addiction, marriage difficulties, repressed childhood issues, or struggles with sexual identity.

When Nate presented the idea of the Samson Society in a morning service at our church, I immediately introduced myself and told him I was with him one hundred percent.

Whatever issue a man carries into my office, I usually recommend that he seek out other men to be accountable to. Tragically, not many Christian groups or programs allow a guy to get really honest.

I was present at the very first meeting of the Society, and it was great. But as the weeks passed, I kept waiting for the elders to burst into the room some Monday night screaming, "We cannot allow this much honesty within the church!" How refreshing it was to have a safe place within my community of faith.

All my life, anxiety has been a regular companion. But one night as I sat waiting for the Samson meeting to start, I noticed that I wasn't feeling anxious at all, but physically at peace. The Samson Society is a place where a man can admit his battle with sin—and name it. It is a place where he can talk about the demons and dragons that have been stalking him for years, about the sexual/physical/verbal abuse he experienced as a kid, about the confusion he felt in a home with two alcoholic parents, or about the shame of wetting the bed until he was seven years old. It is even a place safe enough to speak about the unmentionable subject of same-sex attraction.

There is a power in telling my story in the Samson fellowship. Over time, I have come to see it as part of the greater story of God's restoring work in the world. I have started to understand that I am unique, but I am not strange. As my story connected with the stories of guys I would probably never have met outside of Samson, I found my place in the collective masculinity of the brotherhood. There, in the company of other men, I am affirmed as a man.

In Samson, I know that I am not in competition with the men who sit beside me. I have nothing to prove and neither do they. We are trying to figure out this way of holiness together, honestly admitting our bents and depravities and reminding ourselves each week of who we belong to and whose guidance we seek. We are promise breakers who have tried and failed to do this Christian thing alone, and now we are doing it together.

After two years, the Samson Society is working. My Samson phone and e-mail list is more than a legal page long and contains the names of men who know me, men I can call for anything. I check in with some of them regularly, some even daily.

I have referred a number of men to the Samson Society. Yes, I'm a therapist, but I am also in the Samson Society for myself. After spending my days listening, talking, coaching, and counseling, I look for places to replenish my own soul. Right now, my weekly Samson meeting is the place where God meets me most consistently. He speaks encouragement to me through the lives of other men every week, as friendships are forged across generational lines.

I challenge you to take a chance—visit the Samson Society for a few weeks. But I warn you…you may never leave.

Michael Molloy,
LCSW, ACSW

lifestyle of obsessive self-concern to a growing concern for the woman God had given me to love. This was nothing I could accomplish on my own, but the grace of God channeled through the fellowship of my friends made gradual change possible.

Late one night, three-and-a-half years after I attended my first twelve-step meeting, Allie finally raised the one subject we had never discussed. "I need to know something," she said. "I understand your struggles with pornography. You've told me that you have never had an affair. But I need to know—have you had sex with anyone else since we've been married?"

I froze. *This was it*, the truth I wanted to reveal but dreaded disclosing. I had told counselors and sponsors about my long nightmare with commercial sex, and had talked about it at length with other men. But this was different. Not for a second did I consider lying to Allie, but I hesitated, not wanting to deliver the crushing blow.

Allie waited.

Yes, I finally said, and told her about the prostitutes. With almost clinical detachment, she asked for more information. When did it start? How many were there? What were they like? Were they young? Were they pretty? When was the last time? Had I been tested for sexually transmitted diseases? I answered every question as truthfully as I could, and Allie cried. She kept crying, and I was powerless to comfort her.

Finally, Allie said, "Go away." I went upstairs to the guest bedroom and lay awake most of the night, praying that God would somehow comfort my wife and hoping that Allie, my beautiful Allie, would survive the knowledge of my betrayal.

The next morning I called my sponsor. After listening to my news, he told me he was proud of me for telling the truth when the chips were down. Then he said that my wife, for her own sake, would need to hate me for a while. He said that my job was to allow her to be as angry as she needed to be, for as long as she needed to be angry. He could offer me no guarantees that she would ever love me again.

For the next week, Allie and I barely spoke. Then one afternoon while I was at work, my phone rang. "Here's the thing," Allie said. "It's clear to me now that our marriage was a joke, and I honestly don't think we can fix it. You destroyed whatever we had. I can't even describe how much it hurts to think of you—" She paused for a few seconds, then continued. "But I do realize that you have changed. You are not the man you used to be. I'm willing to start over again with the new you, but it will take some time. I think you should move out for a while. Then we can start dating again, and take it slow from the beginning."

"Okay," I said.

The next day, Allie and I had an appointment with Kaka Ray, a marriage-and-family counselor. I had never met Kaka, but Allie had been seeing her for a few weeks and had already told her about my disclosure. Kaka had agreed to see us together.

After questioning me for about fifteen minutes, Kaka turned to Allie. "Well, what do you want to do from here?" Allie told her about our plan, and Kaka burst out laughing. "I'm sorry," she said. "I'm sure that scenario makes perfect sense to you, but really—move out? Start dating and pretend the past never happened? We can do better than that." She then helped us work out the details of an in-house separation and a series of individual and marriage counseling sessions.

The following year, on our twenty-fifth wedding anniversary, Allie and I renewed our vows. We held the service in the church's historic downtown chapel with Pastor Scotty officiating and rented a nearby restaurant for the reception. Our friends filled the church and the restaurant. All three of our children spoke during the service. Allie had never looked more radiantly beautiful. I felt like the most blessed man alive. Three years later, I still do.

The process of making amends continues. Scarcely a day passes when I don't injure someone, inadvertently or deliberately, in a way that merits some apology. What's more, I still carry a long list of injured people from my past. I am slowly making progress on that list.

Not My Men's Group

Let me begin by making it clear that the Samson Society is not my "men's group." I've been in and out of a lot of those, and to be honest, they never did much for me. I also don't have an "accountability buddy" anymore. I don't go to Samson meetings to get pumped up for God and make a lot of promises I can't keep. Instead, I am now spending my life with a community of men who are no longer willing to tolerate isolation and its effects; guys who have decided to get completely honest about what they've done to themselves and others. We're sharing our stories, sharing our days, going somewhere together. We expect to get beyond the battle and reach the Beauty, but we understand that we are fighting for our hearts, our lives. And we're doing it together. Sounds dramatic, I know. But life is a dramatic story, and the only way for me to get up this mountain is with my brothers.

I've always been a pretty social person. Being around people energizes me, and I learn stuff by speaking out loud and seeing if it sounds true.

My first men's group materialized from a tragedy, as we rallied around a friend in the middle of an ugly divorce so he could vent and we could pray for him. After the crisis passed, we continued to meet for a while, but the group gradually fell apart.

I've also dabbled in men's church fellowships on different occasions over the years, but I have been disappointed by the short-lived enthusiasm of the leadership and the gamesmanship of many men. Some men only attended those meetings to pacify their wives. Others made it clear that they would never drop their guard. After a few semesters of that baloney, I took an "Incomplete" and moved on.

So one Monday night I showed up at a Samson meeting, sick of myself, sick of my patterns and my attachments. I had no real traction in my life. I had figured out my path through the lava, and I was well armored to boot. I was social but alone, connected to a lot of people, but aloof. I realized that I wanted to be perceived as a "caring person." My gifts I had used to advance my cause and myself…frankly, my life was a shallow well, and it hadn't rained in years.

I spoke honestly at my first Samson meeting, but I quickly perceived that I would be out of material soon unless I stopped being a performer. I was stunned by the articulation of struggle and pain, battles and wounds, during the sharing time. These guys weren't screwing around. They wanted to change. *So this is where the brave guys go*, I thought. *This is what a gladiator looks like today*. I called my wife after that first meeting and said, "I found it. Always make me come here."

I've been a part of the Samson Society for a little more than a year now. It has been the best year of my life—and I've had some good ones. I gained the traction I was lacking by listening to the stories of others and discovering my own story. I found the courage to confess my crap when other men were brave enough to trust me with theirs. When I did confess, no one left the room or looked away. They came back the next week and looked me in the eye and loved me well.

After meetings we head down to McCreary's Pub to continue the conversation. It doesn't seem right to go straight home. I usually feel a bit undone. I like to say that at the meeting we take our armor off and at McCreary's we put it back on, one piece (or one pint) at a time. Thinking about my life before Samson is a bit like thinking about life before I had kids. What did I do with my time? I'm sure I wasted a lot. I don't know where this band of brothers is headed, but I know it's better than where I was headed alone. I sure hope we don't screw this thing up. I need it.

Scott Dente

When other guys in Samson ask me about making amends, I give them the same advice I received from my twelve-step friends. I tell them to make their confession and apology as directly and specifically as they can, accepting full responsibility for their actions and refraining from pointing out anything their victim might have done wrong. I warn them not to expect a reciprocal apology, and not to demand understanding or forgiveness. Only when our victims have felt the full pain of our betrayal is it possible for them to forgive us.

Demonstrate Repentance

There are times when the person we injured is not physically available for a direct conversation. In such cases, our Silas may suggest a symbolic way for us to demonstrate our repentance. In other cases, direct amends may be inadvisable for some reason related to the health, safety, or happiness of the person we have harmed. In these cases too, our friends can help us devise an alternative strategy that is spiritually sound.

It is imperative to remember that we are not earning God's forgiveness by making amends. God has forgiven us already through our faith in the restoring work of Christ, and nothing we can ever do will merit his forgiveness. It is also comforting to remember, as we consider our many mistakes, that our heavenly Father has promised to weave even the worst of our failures into his grand story of salvation, to use even our sins and the sins of others for his glory and our ultimate good.

Stage Seven

**I offer myself as a Silas to others. Each day,
I ask God for the grace to seek his kingdom rather than my own,
to serve those he places in my path
rather than serving myself.**

For you are called to freedom, brothers; only don't use this freedom as an opportunity for the flesh, but serve one another through love. For the entire law is fulfilled in one statement: You shall love your neighbor as yourself. (Gal. 5:13–14)

In our meetings we often say that "we in the Samson Society have been set upon a Path, a way of living that leads to godliness and freedom." And it's true. As we journey from stage to stage, climbing the hills and fording the rivers with our brothers, we notice that the landscape is slowly changing, and we are changing too. Our muscles are growing stronger and our burdens lighter, as we fill our lungs with the sweet air of freedom.

When we first set out on this journey, our thoughts were dominated by our own needs, but now as the pilgrimage progresses, we become increasingly alert to the needs of those around us. We are beginning to understand that our comrades need our help as badly as we need theirs. God has entrusted to each of us a gift to be used for the common good, and not one of us is self-sufficient.

When our companions ask for help, our first instinct is probably to offer them our strength, a quick answer, or an inspiring success story. That, indeed, may be what they need, but there is also a paradoxical power in weakness, a strange encouragement that comes from questions echoed and failures shared. Sometimes the greatest gift we can give a brother is to say, "Me too."

J. Silas

At one point near the end of the regular Monday night Samson meetings in Franklin, the meeting leader always asks those who are willing to accept new responsibility as a Silas to raise their hands. By looking around, the newcomers can identify those men who will be receptive to a request for help and guidance. And it isn't just the grizzled old-timers who raise their hands, for we strongly believe that anyone who is walking the Path can serve as a Silas to someone else.

Drunk on Success

After more than fifteen year in the ministry, I considered myself an expert. A church I helped plant had grown to more than 1300 people in four years, and now I was serving as a missionary in Peru with my wife and three kids. Multitudes of people were coming to Christ. My reputation, built on years of sweat and tears, had become my idol, giving me value and significance. I was sacrificing my wife, my children, and myself at its altar.

The harder I worked, the more I left my wife alone—feeling emotionally abandoned, desperate, and betrayed. Oblivious at first, I finally realized I had a critical decision to make: stay on the mission field and lose my marriage, or leave the mission field and keep it.

I left the mission field and brought my family to Tennessee for a time of healing. I had been *drunk on success* for years, selling my soul each day for another bottle of approval, and the extended binge had almost killed my family and me. Now God was giving us a second chance.

Still raw from my ministry experience, I was very distrustful of male friendships, but knew I needed help rebuilding my life. An old acquaintance told me about the Samson Society and I was intrigued. With deliberately low expectations, I met my friend outside the meeting so we could walk in together. We found a room full of normal–looking guys sitting in a circle on folding chairs. Acutely self-conscious, I thought, *If these guys find out what I've been through, they'll think I'm a loser, and they won't want me around.*

The first part of the meeting was a blur until the facilitator said, "Now we've reached the sharing portion of the meeting." Oh no! What a relief when he said, "Let's count off by fives and break into small groups."

I'll never forget the faces of the four other guys in my sharing group that night. They took turns talking and I soon recognized that these guys felt just as vulnerable and exposed as I did. As they spoke, I heard little pieces of my story in their stories. When it came my turn to share, I went for it, giving these guys all the gruesome details. What an unexpected relief when I saw nods and smiles. I had been walking around feeling like a special case, thinking my experience was unique and I was abnormal. I was not alone.

During the final session the facilitator talked about our need for Christian companionship for this leg of our journey, a "Silas," a guy who is flawed and weak like we are, but still willing to hear our story and talk with us a little each day.

The next week I struggled between my need for male companionship and my fear of being betrayed again. But I took a chance and put my name on the list for a Silas. Two or three days later I received a call. I met my Silas at Starbucks and we went for a walk. With startling transparency, he began to share some of his story. Suddenly I felt free to share what was really going on with me. He had given me his armor, and now I felt safe giving him mine.

Sometimes I marvel that I could have been involved in church work for half my life and still missed something as simple and central to the faith as this. Where has true Christian fellowship gone? Authentic fellowship can be found in the Samson Society, and while I don't hear the words mentor or accountability very often, I feel more mentored and accountable as a member of this brotherhood than I have ever felt in over fifteen years of vocational ministry.

Chip Dometri

In fact, nothing supercharges a guy's spiritual life like helping another guy. The Silas role is like a booster rocket. We achieve liftoff on this journey by surrendering to God and seeking the help of another man, and we gain altitude by working our way through the stages of the Path, accepting guidance with humility, and applying ourselves with diligence. But a fresh surge of power comes when we agree to serve as a Silas to someone else. When we make another man's progress our concern, giving him a listening ear and a caring heart and opening ourselves as a conduit for God's grace, we find our walk propelled to a whole new level. We are truly helped by helping, taught by teaching, and encouraged by encouraging.

It is important to understand that a Silas is not a mentor in the way that mentors are normally defined. He is not a Yoda. He has not attended Silas University, is not certified, and is certainly not infallible. A Silas is merely a friend and fellow traveler on the journey of Christian discipleship. He is a guy who calls his own Silas on a regular basis, a guy who is engaged in the ongoing work of the Path. He gathers wisdom from God's Word and the oral tradition of God's people. When you talk to him, he listens and reflects what he hears. He gives suggestions, not orders.

Typically, a Silas will expect *you* to call *him* rather than the other way around. The reasons for this policy are simple and sensible. You need to take responsibility for your own recovery, and you need to learn to ask for help. If your new Silas were to chase you, you'd probably run. Or if he were to take responsibility for initiating every new step in your relationship, you'd probably grow passive. Your Silas may call you from time to time, but usually he will leave the responsibility for initiating contact squarely on your shoulders, where it belongs.

Sometimes at the pub after Samson meetings we trade Silas stories, recounting some of the advice we have received from our helpers. And sometimes we talk about those magical moments when in a conversation with someone who's called us for help, we've heard the Spirit of God speaking in our own voice. This kind of storytelling is a vital part of communal discipleship, multiplying personal experience for the benefit of the group.

We're also moving our conversations about the Silas relationship (and other issues too) onto the Internet. Samson guys are increasingly using subscriber lists, discussion boards, and forums to pose questions and offer insights related to our common life. You can join some of these conversations by googling "Samson discussion" or by visiting www.samsonsociety.org.

Serve Others

When we remember, many of us begin our day with a prayer for usefulness. Then as the day rolls by, we keep our eyes open for opportunities to advance God's kingdom by serving those he places in our path. As we respond with growing obedience to the promptings of the Spirit, we begin to detect evidence of design in our days. Encounters we might earlier have written off to chance turn out to be pregnant with purpose. What was once merely routine becomes extraordinary. Our past failures and other painful memories we have long considered liabilities are somehow transformed into gifts worthy of sharing with others.

And we do not serve alone, for we are coming to understand what it means to belong to a body. Our obedience is strengthened and supported by those around us, the members of Christ's body to whom we are joined and with whom we live in harmony. A profound change is taking place. No longer loners, we are learning to love God and serve him as he always intended—together.

The Strongest Man Alive

I came to the Samson Society hoping to become the strongest man alive, and perhaps a little afraid that someone would eventually try to cut off my hair. Neither happened, but what did has been no less dramatic.

Initially I thought the Samson Society might give me some helpful hints for facing life's challenges as both a husband and daddy, but I soon discovered some of the guys were as messed up as I was, and others were simply too confused to know that their lives were better than mine.

But a funny thing happened in that strange collection of misfits, those guys who didn't dispense hints or scripted anecdotes or memory verses about how we were supposed to conduct our lives. There emerged a strength that only comes from weakness, honesty, and simple faith.

In fact, attempting to build my own strength has been the very source of all kinds of problems in my life. If I'm at the helm of virtually any aspect of my life, if I'm trying to be strong on my own, the inevitable outcome is limitless and profound failure. This reality is inescapable: if I want strength, I must find it in community. If I want to trudge my own way alone through the minefield of our culture, I can do that too.

The Samson Society has a great many lessons for those who are openhearted and humble enough to receive them. For me, it is a safe harbor for the broken man that I was, and the healed man that I am becoming. In an overchurched Southern culture that is often preoccupied with preserving pretenses, the Samson Society is a rare and special place for me to be real.

Neal Grizzell

⚑ Twelve ⚑

Our Contract
An Annotated Summary of the Pact

NEAR THE END OF EVERY SAMSON MEETING WE READ THE Pact, a list of seven principles under which our Society operates. We take the time to read the Pact at every meeting because each of us belongs to other groups where the rules are different, and the only way to keep ourselves from slipping unconsciously into familiar patterns is to remind ourselves regularly of Samson's distinctives.

Without the Pact, the Samson Society would eventually become a denomination, a corporation, or a cult—or it would self-destruct through turf wars, power politics, and scandal. Because the Society is full of human beings it will always have its troubles, but the provisions of the Pact provide a measure of protection against our worst impulses.

I will close my description of the Samson Society, therefore, with a quick summary of the Pact, offering a bit of personal commentary on each of its articles.

Article One

**God is the sole owner of the Samson Society
and its only authority.
No member may speak for the entire Society.**

A few months ago, a visitor to the Monday night Samson meeting introduced himself by saying, "I'm Dan, and I'm here because I've never joined a cult before." That line got a good laugh, but for me the humor was a little unsettling. I found myself wondering whether people actually suspect the Samson Society of being a cult. Not that I would blame anyone for being suspicious. I'm suspicious, too, whenever I see a highly motivated religious group whose members seem to spend a lot of time together. I start wondering how much freedom the group actually allows, who's really in charge of things, and what their ultimate goal is. It's a caution born of experience, for in my life I've been around a number of groups that could be accurately classified as cults.

In my mind, one of the first indications that a group might be a cult is the dominating presence of a single human personality, a leader whose words are regarded as uniquely inspired and whose orders are followed without question. Such a group belongs to its leader. No decision may be made without his endorsement, and his pronouncement on every issue, no matter how trivial, is considered authoritative. Even if the founder is long dead, the group reveres him, elevating his ideas to the level of Scripture and seeking to find its way forward by the light of his genius.

That's why, in every one of our meetings, we make it a point to reiterate that "*God* is the sole owner of the Samson Society and its only authority." And to make the point even clearer, we explicitly declare, "No member may speak for the entire Society."

Please understand that this book is subject to this rule. Even though I was one of the guys who got the Society rolling in the first place, Samson does not belong to me, and my words do not carry unique authority. I've written the *first* book about the Society, but certainly not the *last* one and hopefully not the *best* one. Our common understanding of the journey will grow deeper as we go, and others who join our ranks in the future will explain the principles of the Society more eloquently than I can. Flaws in what I have written will become apparent with time, but other members of the Society will correct them. Together we will respect God's ownership of this enterprise, acknowledging the supreme authority of Holy Scripture and the guiding presence of the Holy Spirit.

Here in Franklin, where my friends have spent enough time with me to learn my defects and limitations, it's easy for them keep this principle in mind. Whenever my interest in the group becomes too proprietary or I overstep my bounds by making some sort of pronouncement or promise on the Society's behalf, they balk, and someone pointedly asks, "Nate, are you speaking for the entire Society?" Whenever that happens I am forced by the Pact to retreat in the direction of humility and sanity, reminding myself again that God is the sole owner of the Samson Society and its *only* authority.

Article Two

**All members of the Society are equals,
friends and fellow servants, bound by love and honor.
No member may command the obedience of another.**

The second article of the Pact is related to the first, but it carries the radical nature of our relationships even further. Not only does the Samson Society lack a human leader; it also lacks a *hierarchy*.

As I pointed out earlier in this book, Jesus warned his disciples against emulating the authority madness of the unbelieving world, the preoccupation with power that produces arrogance and self-indulgence in governors, and resentment and passivity in the governed. God has instituted *roles* in the church, of course—elder and deacon, apostle, teacher, and more—but the New Testament emphasizes that these roles are designed for service, not privilege, and Jesus said that the person who wants to be great in the kingdom must become the servant of all.

Over the centuries, the church has responded to the challenge of church government in many ways, developing episcopal forms of leadership, apostolic forms, oligarchic forms, prophetic forms, and congregational forms. A scriptural case can be made for each of these

Samson Comes to California

My friend John Lohr called to tell me that twenty-four men were making the long trip from Tennessee to the central coast of California just to hold some kind of meeting in our gym. He said I ought to stick around after our monthly men's breakfast and check it out. *Why did he call me?* I wondered. *I'm overcommitted and under the weather.*

During the breakfast I started taking inventory of the other men:

- musicians I've led worship with
- contractors I've bent "mission trip nails" with
- surfers I've scrubbed manly breakfast pans with
- guys who know me as "Dave-the-shrink"
- professional men whose suicidal kids have sat in my office
- husbands I've guided though many a family crisis
- emotionally broken guys I've counseled back together
- lonely, depressed, and isolated men I've listened to through long dark nights

and *me*, a composite of all of them and more—or today, less.

While we scraped dishes, a group of strange guys began arranging chairs in a large oval in the gym.

The program began with worship, then a speaker talked transparently about his own needs and failures, comparing himself with the biblical character Samson. The speaker said he was called by God, but the absence of honest friends had doomed him to isolation and despair. His solution? Something called the Samson Society.

Then the group meeting began. "Today's topic is fear," the leader announced, as we broke into smaller groups.

There were five guys in my breakout group. Three of them were from Tennessee. One by one, they poured themselves out, speaking to us like old and trusted friends. Their honesty and humility pulled the plug on my tank of churning emotions and racing thoughts. Out came words I wasn't prepared to hear myself say: "I'm afraid I'm really close to losing it—at home, at work, at this church, with those I call my friends, and especially my wife and daughter. I can see it, hear it, and feel it coming. I'm scared."

I had been doing individual and group therapy every day for thirty years, listening to others and giving them my full attention, but I couldn't remember the last time a man had stopped to *really listen to me*, caring enough to hear me out. I vented a full five minutes. When I was finished, nobody rescued me from my words. They just sat with me, giving me affirmation and respect, allowing my raw feelings to hang in the air. And then a wonderful thing happened. I could sense the presence of the Holy Spirit in our little circle of believers, and I could feel my fear lifting. Five guys. Five stories. Thirty minutes of healing.

Within ten days of that divinely appointed Saturday breakfast, more than thirty men were holding Samson Society meetings in two different locations in our town. Our groups are still in their infancy, but relationships are growing deeper every week. Silas relationships are forming. Men are calling each other multiple times daily, offering support and encouragement. This is not shame-based accountability or legalistic reporting, but real men finding real love and spiritual connection in fresh and practical ways.

After nearly fifty years of believing in Jesus and trying my best to "be like him," I am finally on my way to becoming the man, husband, father, counselor, minister, brother, and friend that God created me to be—not by self-help, but by his powerful presence in the lives of my brothers in a real Christian community.

Dave Mayfield
San Luis Obispo, CA

systems, and individual members of the Samson Society can operate within any of them. Because we are *Christians* first and foremost, members of the Church Universal, we can submit in good conscience to servant leadership in any ecclesiastical system. We can gladly lend our passion and muscle to the work of the local congregation in which God has planted us, supporting the efforts of pastor or council, board or bishop. But *within the Samson Society* there is no hierarchy at all. No man among us is permitted to command the obedience of another.

To say that we do not have an authority structure does not mean that nobody in the Society carries any authority. Quite the contrary. We are all fully authorized to promulgate the principles of the Society as we understand them, as the seventh article of the Pact makes clear. What's more, even though the Society does not give any member coercive power over any other, any member may voluntarily grant authority to someone he trusts, someone who has earned that trust by demonstrating integrity, humility, and selfless service. And he may rescind that authority anytime his trust is violated.

There are men in the Samson Society whose words carry great weight because of the way they live. These guys are not always the brightest or the best educated, the socially prominent or the most "successful." They may not appear outwardly religious, and they certainly are not perfect. What sets them apart is the congruence of their rhetoric with the reality of their conduct. They are seekers after truth, and they are committed to obeying the truth as God grants them the vision and ability to do so.

But even these authoritative guys do not form an upper class in the Samson Society. If there's one thing we've learned in our meetings, it's that God often speaks through the unlikeliest of instruments. He is as capable of addressing us today through the ramblings of a newcomer as through the measured pronouncements of a veteran. And even if the newcomer speaks nothing but nonsense, he is still a brother, a bearer of God's image and worthy of respect. His brokenness is a gift to the fellowship. In due time his special aptitudes and insights will become apparent. For now he needs to know that we consider him an equal, and if he wants to join our band, we will tie our common life to his with bonds of love and honor.

Article Three

The Society owns no property, collects no dues or fees, pays no salaries, incurs no debts.

This article of the Pact concerns three subjects that often expose my own spiritual immaturity: property, money, and debt. Even though I am a man who loves God and is committed to following Christ, I sometimes go too far to acquire property and protect it. I sometimes neglect others and myself to make money. And I have been known to incur debt lightly, momentarily forgetting that the borrower becomes the lender's slave.

I'm not alone, of course. The history of the church is replete with stories of vibrant Spirit-led communities that were undone—neutralized—by incorrect attitudes regarding property, money, or debt. Some of them embarked on grand expansion schemes and then succumbed to failure or "success." Others, in the ebb and flow of income and annual budgets, were torn apart by greed. And some communities foolishly attempted to transcend their limitations by incurring debts that wound up costing them their ministry. That's why this protective provision is included in the Pact.

All of us in the Samson Society wrestle daily with the realities of property, money, and debt in our personal lives. Some of us take our financial issues to our Silas or our personal team of advisors, receiving wisdom and strength from our brothers. We also make it a habit to extend financial help in times of crisis. Occasionally our group in Franklin has gathered voluntary contributions to meet a special need. We do not collect an offering during a standard meeting, however. The Samson Society does not have a treasurer or a bank account, and we will never assess any dues or fees. Our fellowship is free.

God's Not Angry with Me Anymore..

Fortunately, I was blessed with an exceptional memory. I can remember events that occurred well before I was three years old. For example, I can remember my mother "leading me to the Lord"—letting me know that I did "bad" things and needed Jesus to die for my "bad things" and forgive me—before I turned three. And my memory is not limited to events. I can also remember emotions and attitudes from those toddler years, a gift that psychologists say is rare.

One of the earliest emotions I can remember is anger. I was surrounded by Christians, but everyone was angry. My parents were angry—angry at smokers and drinkers, angry at Hollywood and movie makers, angry at me for not being potty trained and talking too loud and too much, angry at my baby brother for getting into things all the time. My church was also angry—angry at women in pants and makeup in the workplace, angry at the communists and the hippies and the rock 'n' roll musicians and the Democrats and the liberal "ecumenical" churches.

Naturally, I imagined God was angry too. After all, wasn't he busy trampling out the vintages of the "grapes of wrath"? God was angry at all the sinners of the world. In my mind, God was an old man in the sky pointing a bony finger at me and saying, "I'm going to get you, my precious, and your little dog too!"

When I reached adolescence, God was angry at me for "letting" myself be sexually abused by ten different men and teenagers on the mission field where we lived. God was angry at me for looking at the *Playboy* magazines in my guitar teacher's studio. God was angry at me for tasting my first beer and making out with girls, or when I wanted to play softball instead of going to youth group. God's anger was endless.

Later, theological enlightenment helped, but it couldn't

fully correct my "Angry God" concept. Jack Miller pointed me in the right direction when he said, "Cheer up! You're much worse than you think, but Jesus is a much bigger Savior than you ever dared imagine." I heard about a gracious God who gives me a righteousness that is not my own or based on any element of my performance. I came to understand the love of God *intellectually*, but *emotionally* that radical love takes a long, long, *long* time to sink in.

For years, the church still seemed like an angry place to me. I couldn't bear to face that anger. I couldn't dare admit, therefore, that I had been severely abused as a child and adolescent. I couldn't dare admit that I had a four-year affair with the wife of a close friend while in professional ministry. I couldn't dare admit that I struggled with depression and alcohol abuse and sometimes was so angry at God that I doubted his very existence even while preparing to lead the Sunday worship service.

Then along came Samson. In the Samson Society, I found a group of men who are brutally honest without judging one another. These men believe that we are all sinner-saints, and the process of sanctification includes recovery from our various addictions. They show the unconditional love of our Father by standing by me no matter what I do, but they are not afraid to challenge my lies and confront my unbelief. The Samson Society is a band of "pirate monks" that I can laugh with, cry with, pray with, drink with, cuss with—and they are helping me to understand that God really isn't angry with me anymore.

No, Samson is not some miracle cure, but a community that has recognized that sanctification is a work of God's grace, accomplished by his Spirit through the community of faith. Here it is safe to confess our sins and struggles to each other, pray for one another, and support each other in reality rather than denial. As Brennan Manning said, "Wholeness is brokenness acknowledged and thereby healed."

Matt Creamer

That's not to say that there is no room in the Samson Society for profit. The seventh article of the Pact says that individual members of the Society may create and distribute, freely *or for profit*, personal explanations and applications of the Society's principles. This provision allows those who are heavily engaged in the work of the Society to be supported by their work. But the Pact also assures that responsibility for supporting a man will never fall upon the Society itself, and that our fellowship will never develop a bureaucracy or a professional class.

In the future, teams of Samson guys may create various business entities that support the work of the Society, but those entities will always be distinct and completely separate from the Society itself. The Samson Society will never hire an executive director, build a corporate headquarters, or compile an annual budget. And it will never take out a loan.

No property. No dues. No fees. No salaries. No debt.

Weird, huh?

Article Four

**The Society is an extension of the Church Universal.
It is not a corporate entity and can make no contracts
with congregations, denominations, causes, or campaigns,
regardless of their merit.**

Samson meetings are popping up in unexpected places these days. Two weeks ago, for example, the visiting father of one of our local Samson guys told me that he has already started a Samson group in Denton, Texas. Yesterday I heard about a new pastors-only Samson meeting that has started up in Atascadero, California. These and other new groups seem to cross all denominational lines: Presbyterian, Baptist, Nazarene, Methodist, charismatic, Assemblies of God, Catholic, Church of Christ, Episcopalian, and a number of nondenominational churches are already well represented in the Samson Society. And men who have no formal church affiliation are finding their place too.

I'm thrilled by every new piece of news, but lately I've been getting a little nervous too, plagued by the uneasy feeling that some of us may be taking this whole thing a little too far.

A few days ago a random comment by an enthusiastic Samson convert put my fears in focus. This guy, a young junior minister, was telling me about his vision for promoting the Society in the large church where he works. "This Samson thing is the *real deal!*" he said, his eyes flashing with excitement. "*Everybody* needs it! The Samson Society is . . ." He searched for a moment for the right description, and smiled when he found it. "The Samson Society is *new wine!*"

As you probably know, *new wine* is a biblical term. Jesus employed it in a conversation with the Pharisees, an exchange the apostle Luke recorded in his gospel. In response to questions about the controversial behavior of his disciples, Jesus said:

No one puts new wine into old wineskins. Otherwise, the new wine will burst the skins, it will spill, and the skins will be ruined. But new wine should be put into fresh wineskins. And no one, after drinking old wine, wants new, because he says, "*The old is better.*" (Luke 5:37–39, emphasis added)

Jesus wasn't exactly talking about the Samson Society when he made these observations, but I do believe the passage contains principles that apply to us, principles vital to the growth of the Society and the protection of the whole church.

The first principle is contained in Jesus's observation that *for people who have been drinking it for a while, old wine tastes better than the new stuff.*

New wine is fun, effervescent, and unpredictable. The wine-pressing festival is a joyous time, and the taste of new wine is sweet for those involved in producing it. But even the best new wine gets better with age. Wine grows sweeter and stronger with time.

The Samson Society is fun and exciting at this very early stage in its development, but it is also unstable. Our fellowship is sweet, but it will grow sweeter as it matures. Our teaching is strong, but it will grow stronger. And for now, we who love the taste of new wine must always remember that *not everyone enjoys it as much as we do*. We shouldn't be shocked or offended when a Christian turns up his nose at the Samson Society. For anyone who has acquired a taste for old wine, that reaction is perfectly normal and eminently sensible.

Yes, the Samson Society is an authentic work of God, but it is not the first thing God has ever done in the church. God has been faithful to his people in every generation. He has done many "new" things in the past. Every tribe in Christendom traces its beginnings to an exciting work of God, a fresh outpouring that was thrilling and controversial in its day. For many Christians, yesterday's new wine has become today's fine wine. Those people are connoisseurs. They know what they like. They know that their old wine is good, and they regard as ignorant anyone who tries to tell them that some brand of new wine is better than the vintage they've been savoring for years.

The second thing we must remember is that *old wineskins are fragile*. Yes, the wine they contain has improved with age, becoming more nuanced and complex with every passing year, but that maturity has been accompanied by a loss of flexibility in the container. Old containers must be handled carefully, with great respect. They certainly shouldn't be emptied of their precious contents and filled with rambunctious new wine. Such an act would be more than traumatic; it would be sacrilegious.

A great many churches have been split by the reckless introduction of new wine. Arrogant reformers who forced everybody to drink the latest draught have irreparably damaged many good Christians. Whenever that happens, a double tragedy ensues. The old wineskins are ruined, and the new wine is spilled.

That's why the fourth article of our Pact is so vitally important. Some Samson men suppose that this provision, which prohibits the Society from making any contracts with congregations, denominations, causes, or campaigns, is intended to protect the Society from local church politics and denominational squabbles. That, indeed, is partly its intent. But another vital purpose of this article is to protect old wineskins from the disruptive influence of new wine, to safeguard and honor existing churches by preventing anyone from imposing our Society on them. If we adhere faithfully to this principle, no church will ever be split by a disagreement over the Samson Society.

It is my hope that the Samson Society will bring the experience of Christian community to men who have long languished inside the church or who have drifted away from it. Paradoxically, we can only realize this hope if we maintain a certain independence, resisting every impulse to impose our way of life upon the good lovers of old wine.

Article Five

**Any two or more persons who believe the Fact,
who agree to follow this Path and join this Pact,
may initiate a meeting of the Samson Society.**

Any two Christian guys who understand the Path and are committed to walking it together can start a Samson meeting. They don't need to secure permission from anyone in the Society to do it. Nobody from Samson headquarters is going to give them any grief, because Samson headquarters doesn't exist.

Why at least two guys? Because in the Samson Society, we don't do anything alone. If a guy were to get a meeting started all by himself, he'd probably become the Grand Pooh-bah of the thing. Then if the meeting went well, the success would go straight to his head, and if it went poorly, he'd sink into the depths of despair and there'd be nobody around to pull him out of it.

This doesn't mean that *only* two guys can start a meeting. The bigger the beginning core of leaders, the better. Based on our experience here in Franklin, I'd say that a dozen guys in the founding group is probably optimal. We've also found, at least for us, that a group needs to think about planting a new group when attendance reaches about

Why Go Deep?

Unlike a lot of other guys, I didn't show up at the Samson Society looking for friends, adventure, or a band of brothers. I came out of curiosity. I love being "in the know" about things, and I started thinking I might be missing out on something.

I have joined a few Christian men's groups in my day, and not one of them was able to change me. Those groups basically stayed at a social level. They encouraged conformity, discouraging any authenticity that made others uncomfortable. Subtly and overtly, those groups pressured guys to ignore or deny their deepest needs, wants, doubts, affections, and pain.

I can vividly recall the complete discomfort I felt at my first Samson meeting. I noticed the difference as soon as I walked into the room. Instead of handshakes and shoulder-punches, I saw guys embracing and greeting one another warmly. I thought, *These guys are excited to see each other!*

When my turn came to state my name and reason for attending the meeting, I fumbled and stuttered, my heart in my mouth. As the attention of the room moved to the next guy, I suddenly felt acutely self-aware. That happens a lot at Samson.

Breaking out into small groups did not ease my anxiety. I think the topic was *trust*, and I decided there was no way I'd speak up first. In fact, I soon perceived that by listening to others I could glean good insight and relevant information that would allow me to appear self-possessed and articulate when I spoke.

I might have been able to protect that image if I hadn't made one simple promise to myself before my next Samson meeting. I promised that this time there would be no baloney.

On that second week, all my polished sound bites and hastily rehearsed bullet points shattered, and I came unglued. I don't recall exactly what I said, but I spoke the truth about myself, and it felt good. Actually, "good" is an understatement. It felt like an enormous weight had been lifted from my shoulders. And it had. I had opened my load to every man in that room, and one by one they had taken all the stones I had been carrying around all by myself. They also helped relieve me of the shame and condemnation that had multiplied the weight of my besetting sin. What a feeling!

Almost immediately, I felt the urge to carry something for someone else. I started *really* listening to others, sharing their concerns, encouraging them, crying with them, laughing with them, and—most importantly of all—loving them without criticism or condemnation.

I now know that brothers can help us find a path through the pain of our past and the brokenness it has caused. Our damaged lives can be made beautiful. Through friendships that are honest and whole, God's amazing grace can produce real change.

I often encourage first-time Samson visitors to attend three meetings before deciding whether the group is right for them. The first meeting goes fast, the second makes more sense, but by the third meeting, most guys wonder why they didn't come sooner. They may still feel a little nervous. After all, knowing that your life is going to change can be pretty intimidating. But as General Eric Shinseki said, "If you don't like change, you're going to like irrelevance even less." I am grateful that we are not irrelevant to God. He is changing the hearts and lives of men through the Samson Society, and I'm honored to be one of them.

Jack Wallin

forty-five to fifty. It's difficult to create a top-quality community experience in just an hour with a group much bigger than that.

Before I suggest a strategy for starting a new meeting, let me make crystal clear what I *don't* recommend. I don't recommend a splashy top-down start, a kickoff announcement from the pulpit that (ta-*dah!*) the Samson Society is the church's new ministry for men. Such a start is practically doomed to failure. Most men cannot be pushed, and those who are forced into participating in a Samson group often react to the experience with suspicion or baffled indifference. If denied an alternative, they may become antagonistic. Two simple truths are inescapable: *Samson is not for everyone,* and *Good things grow slowly.* In order to build a strong and durable fellowship, we must first abandon our one-size-fits-all mentality and our ambitions for overnight stadium-filling success. Humbly and patiently, we must build real relationships with men who are ripe for them. Our fellowship grows better by attraction than promotion.

My own observation has convinced me that it is very difficult for a pastor to serve as the driving force behind the formation of a Samson Society group in his own church. While the new group does need the pastor's endorsement, his habit of taking the lead in any church-related activity will probably delay the emergence of an egalitarian ethos if he plays a highly visible role in it. Even if he subordinates his urge to teach and lead, his parishioners will instinctively give the pastor's words more weight than their own, and his presence in the meeting may inhibit honesty. In my opinion, it is usually best for the pastor to join a Samson group in another church, a group where he can experience the freedom of being just an ordinary guy among friends. In new groups, leadership should come first from those who are not instantly recognized as religious professionals.

How should you go about starting a new meeting of the Samson Society? If you are alone, I recommend praying first for a potential Silas, someone who can serve as your fellow laborer in the task. God will surely lead you to the man, and the two of you can set out on the Path together. If you've never experienced a fellowship like the one described in this book, I also recommend doing your best to visit an existing Samson Society group or participate in an online meeting at www.samsonsociety.org.

Next I suggest giving this book to your pastor and asking him to read it. Unless he has been cloistered away in his study, your pastor already knows some men who are privately struggling with problems fueled by isolation, guys who need a safe friend. If he supports your vision, he may be willing to pass your name and phone number along to a few of those men and suggest that they call you. He may also be willing to introduce you to other local caregivers such as counselors, social workers, and other clergy who might be willing to send guys in your direction.

At our church, Pastor Scotty regularly peppers his sermons with references to the Samson Society, and our weekly meetings are listed in the church bulletin. When my friends and I are called upon to describe the Society to various groups within the church, we describe it as a mutual aid society for men, a safe place to be completely honest, a great place to make friends. This kind of exposure, together with the person-to-person contacts we all make in our neighborhoods and workplaces, brings a steady stream of visitors through the doors of our Monday night meeting.

When you launch your new meeting, you can register it instantly at www.samsonsociety.org, a Web site created and administered by Samson volunteers. Free downloads, such as the charter and the meeting format, are also available on the site. The site allows members to leave feedback about any meeting they visit. That way any meetings that drift from the essentials of the charter can be identified by other members and removed from the directory, if necessary.

It is important to bear in mind, however, that the Samson Society encourages diversity. Only the charter must remain unchanged—every other piece of Samson culture is up for improvement. For example, the meeting format described in this book is not sacrosanct. Anyone is welcome to try his hand at writing a better one. Some guys have already produced good alternative formats for different kinds of Samson meetings, including feedback/discussion meetings, speaker meetings, and meetings specifically designed for teens. My advice: launch your meeting using a format that has already been used successfully by others—then after you've gotten the thing rolling, make any adjustments necessary to get it firing on all cylinders. Capitalize on the creativity of your brothers, and then add your own twist. When you find something that works, share it.

Article Six

**We hold in strictest confidence
any personal information shared by other members,
unless permission to divulge it is given
by any whom its disclosure might affect.**

Most first-time visitors to our local Samson meeting are stunned by the level of honesty in our sharing times. We don't require anyone to say anything, of course, and any guy who does decide to take the floor is free to speak in code, if he wants to, or even to blather on about theology or self-improvement if he thinks that will help. Before long, however, most guys choose to speak the truth about themselves. And after leaping from that bridge for the first time, they find that authenticity is exhilarating. They get a taste of the freedom that comes from walking in the light, and they begin to experience the bond that forms between men who are living openly with each other.

Men find themselves saying things in Samson meetings that many of them have never said out loud before—certainly never in church. And I'm not just talking about confessions. In fact, most Samson confessions are made privately, in one of those daily conversations between a man and his Silas. No, I'm talking about an honest expression of a man's feelings, his real doubts and fears, those deeply burning questions that do not yield easily to simple answers.

Our meetings foster this kind of honesty by removing the programmed "Christian" group responses that routinely kill honesty. Let's face it: the reason many guys have stopped telling the truth in church is because most churches actively discourage truthfulness. Even in Christian men's groups, the cost of candor is usually painfully high, the punitive response to it swift and decisive.

You've probably seen that poor fellow who decided one day to be honest in a Christian meeting. Maybe he'd been caught in a sin, so he really had nothing left to lose, or perhaps he was so plagued by guilt that he decided to take the church's rhetoric about grace and forgiveness at face value and bare his soul in a desperate bid for freedom.

I remember a guy who did that. As soon as the fateful words were uttered he looked around, hoping somebody would say, "Me too," but all he heard were crickets. After a pause, a curious investigator launched into spiritual cross-examination. Then a few concerned "ex-sinners" gathered around him and preached a series of sermons disguised as prayers. Finally, a helpful brother prescribed three Scripture verses to be taken in the morning and at bedtime. Later, the guy was assigned to a probation officer—excuse me, an "accountability partner"—who would check in on him for a few weeks to make sure he had actually turned around.

In all this religious activity, he heard this message loud and clear: "You have lost status, boy. For the foreseeable future, you can forget about being a leader in this group, or even a trusted member. Maybe later, if you can demonstrate that you have been fully rehabilitated and if you promise never to speak that way again, we will consider reinstating your membership."

To make matters worse, as he left the meeting that poor guy was struck by the realization that he had just volunteered to become the church's new topic of conversation. Suddenly he knew that telephone lines were already humming with the latest "prayer request." Next Sunday, his suspicions were confirmed. The sidelong glances, the awkward silences, the careful distances kept by his former associates, their wives, and others, verified that his disclosure was now common currency in the congregation.

No wonder most Samson rookies wait a few weeks before bringing

It's Kinda Like Sushi...

God directed me to Samson through a pastor and a counselor who both suggested that I "check it out." I was a little skeptical at first. My pride said that the group probably wasn't for me, at least not for long, but by the third meeting I was hooked. That week when it came my turn to introduce myself, I said, "This is my new addiction. It's kinda like sushi—you have to try it more than once to like it."

I originally went to Samson to deal with my struggle with pornography and the chasm it helped create between my wife and me. When I heard other guys talk about the same struggle, I started to see that the enemy had been lying to me for years, saying, "You're the only one in the world with this struggle. You're weird, a pathetic failure, and no one will understand your secret." Samson was the first place I ever talked about the problem in a setting that was public but confidential. To this day I have not felt an ounce of shame from anyone in the group, nor has my disclosure come back to bite me through gossip. The confidentiality of the group, the knowledge that I can trust these guys, has made it possible for me to be completely honest.

Another painful area of my life is the current state of my marriage. My wife and I have been separated for the past ten months, and she has filed for divorce. We have three children who desperately want us back together as a family. I desire that too. Being able to share my pain, sorrow, and frustration with men who understand it has been invaluable. My Silas went through a similar experience, but God resurrected his marriage and he is now happily married. He has allowed me to lament my frustrations, desires, and pain, and he has helped me to see God more and more through this trial. It is safe to say that God put me together with my Silas. I didn't know him before

Samson, but he heard my story one Monday night and chose to engage me.

I am proud to tell our kids that their dad belongs to the Samson Society. I explain that the meetings give me a safe place to talk things over with other men. I hope one day I can share this experience with my wife and let her see how it is changing me.

I hate missing Samson—ever. In the Society I see a level of trust between men that I have never experienced before, the kind of trust that guys build when they fight side-by-side in battle. Even though we don't wear uniforms and carry rifles, we are together in the battle of life. There isn't a guy in the group I wouldn't help if he called on me.

Gaining strength and freedom from this experience has given me the desire to become a Silas for someone else. I know I'm not an expert or better than anyone else. We are all equals, sinner-saints, pirate monks. I think I am beginning to see Jesus for the first time in my life through the lives of other men who refuse to put on the "happy face" and only shoot the breeze about sports, the weather, and their jobs. Guys have helped me by being real, and I want to give the same help to someone else.

I expect to be a member of the Samson Society for as long as I am alive. (Hey, there are no dues, so why not?) God has already blessed me in ways I never thought possible through these guys, and I believe there is much more blessing to come, whatever the future brings.

Tom White

their full weight to the meeting. This is a Christian fellowship, after all, and experience has taught them to be very guarded around Christians.

But gradually the newcomer begins to believe that Samson really is a safe environment. He notices, for example, that every guy is given the opportunity to speak in the meeting without interruption or rebuttal, a period of time Scott Dente calls "the sacred seven minutes," during which no one is allowed to correct him, instruct him, or question him. During this sharing time, every man is encouraged to speak the truth about himself, to say out loud what he's doing and feeling and learning. He is also encouraged to share his experience, strength, and hope *without fixing anyone*, and to listen respectfully to any other man who chooses to speak.

Making the adjustment to this kind of discipleship can be difficult for men who have spent a lot of time in churches that are focused on dispensing "fixes." Such men may have a hard time understanding that our habit of correcting others can actually force our targets into lifelong patterns of dependency or dishonesty. Sometimes the best way to help a guy is to surround him with the love and support of a community—and then allow him to grapple with his own problems.

Because this philosophy is so dramatically different from "normal" church thinking, some critics have suggested that it is subchristian—or maybe unchristian. But actually the Samson model of discipleship is very consistent with biblical guidelines. Consider, for example, this instruction about community and personal responsibility that the apostle Paul gave to the first-century Christians in Galatia:

> Carry one another's burdens; in this way you will fulfill the law of Christ. For if anyone considers himself to be something when he is nothing, he is deceiving himself. But each person should examine his own work, and then he will have a reason for boasting in himself alone, and not in respect to someone else. For each person will have to carry his own load. (Gal. 6:2–5)

During every one of our meetings, we take pains to stress the confidentiality of the group. When the Pact is read aloud, several men usually join in on article six, boisterously adding their voices to its key phrase: *"strictest confidence!"*

What does "strictest confidence" mean? It means that while we might tell somebody else that a guy made a courageous contribution during the sharing time—something like, "Our group was great. Joe really brought it tonight"—we never disclose the substance or details of a guy's sharing outside the group without his permission. We don't tell our wives or girlfriends about the personal information disclosed, and we certainly don't include that information in the book we're writing about the Samson Society.

Obviously a disclosure made in a group is no longer completely private. It's possible that a rookie or a visitor might mishandle information gathered in that setting. For that reason every man should carefully consider what he shares in a group, just as Allie and I prayerfully weighed the risks and rewards of transparency before I told my story in this book. Remember—it is possible to tell the truth without telling the whole truth. Details are not always necessary.

Still, we do need to disclose the ugly details to someone, and that someone is usually our Silas, the trustworthy companion we selected for this stretch of the road. If we are well matched with our Silas, we find that we are able tell him everything. We don't weigh him down by describing every painful episode in our life, especially since, like *Seinfeld*, most of our episodes are reruns. But we are careful to tell him the most shameful ones. In doing so, we expose our secrets to the light of God's grace and the healing power of the body of Christ. And healing does come—just as the apostle James promised it would:

Confess your sins to one another and pray for one another, so that you may be healed. (James 5:16)

For this kind of deep honesty to develop between a man and his Silas, strict confidentiality is absolutely essential. To emphasize my pledge of confidentiality to those I serve as a Silas, I'll sometimes ask a guy to write down his most shameful and vivid memories; then, after he's read them aloud to me and we've talked and prayed about them, we will ceremonially burn them. After all, God has forgotten them. My friend may still need to take some steps to deal with the consequences of his sin, such as making amends for damage he has caused, but God has already forgiven and forgotten his transgressions. I can try to do the same. Whether I can succeed in forgetting them or not, I promise never to breathe a word about them to anyone.

To be sure, serving as someone's Silas can test your patience. While we all know—or say we know—that God continues to forgive our repeated failures, most of us find it difficult to maintain that kind of forbearance to others for an extended length of time, especially if we have fallen into the trap of thinking that we are responsible for "fixing" our companions.

If a man who has asked me for help does not respond quickly enough to my suggestions for change, I may be tempted to start applying pressure. I may even threaten to disclose his secret struggle to someone else inside or outside the fellowship, perhaps misapplying Matthew 18:15–17 to justify my actions. (In that passage, Jesus did not give rules for confronting *any* sinner, but for resolving conflict with someone who has sinned "against you.")

Exposing someone else's sin almost always turns out badly. My attempts to assert control over a friend's behavior usually show that I really do not trust the transforming power of God's indwelling Spirit, and they tell my friend that his behavior is more important to me than he is. He may well suspect that I am trying to force him to change so I can feel better—and that's probably true.

I'm not suggesting that my responsibility as a Silas is to affirm the sins of my friend, offering him nothing but sympathy. A good Silas will battle for the heart of his friend. He will ask hard questions, and he will continue to warn against the consequences of destructive behavior. At times, he will plead with his brother to repent. He might even say something like, "Nate, I'm really concerned about this pattern in your life. I worry about its consequences for you and others. I think you need help, more help than I alone can give you. Why don't we call a couple of our mutual friends from the Society in on this one, so we can talk and pray about it together?"

I sometimes encounter resistance to the principle of confidentiality from believers, resistance that I think is often related to weak faith. Here's how I see it. When our faith in Christ wavers, we tend to drift in the direction of self-justifying, performance-based legalism. We start thinking, along with the Pharisees, that we actually possess a right-eousness of our own, a fragile righteousness that can only be maintained by outer cleanliness and a careful segregation from "sinners." We lose sight of our own sin and become fixated on the sins of others. Anytime we're in the company of someone we have identified as a sinner, we can't be kind to him without feeling like an accomplice. And when someone admonishes us to be gracious and patient toward that person, we cry out in genuine alarm, "But that's not grace, that's giving him a license to sin!"

Let's get this straight. Our friend will probably not stop sinning just because I insist upon it. All of us are very capable of sinning without a license. Oh, he may alter his behavior in order to keep my friendship, but even that response betrays his belief that my love for him is conditional, a belief that is fatal to true friendship. In all likelihood, he will start giving me edited versions of his life, reverting to the patterns of lying and secrecy that only make his habit worse.

Does this mean that I must suffer the folly of my friend in silence or walk with him all the way into the jaws of disaster? Certainly not. In fact, I may actually need to part company with an unrepentant friend, temporarily exposing him to the ravages of sin for his own good. (There are a few good reasons to resign as a Silas—this is just one of them.) I may need to say something like, "I will always be your friend, but I cannot go where you are going. The dangers are too great. I fear for you. I will pray for you every day while you are gone, and if you ever decide to turn around, I will rejoin you immediately."

A Pastor's Perspective

Hi, my name is Thomas. I am a member of the Samson Society. I am also a pastor. I'm writing especially to my fellow pastors who might be wondering about this whole Samson business.

I'm always a bit wary when some well-meaning member of my congregation comes up with "the next big thing." Sometimes it's okay, sometimes it's bad, but most of the time it's just something else I have to deal with. Rarely do I come across something new I can genuinely get excited about.

You may not get excited about Samson, and I'm not trying to sell it. But let me do some work for you by asking and answering some of the questions I would ask if I were in your place.

Is the Samson Society in line with my vision for my congregation? That depends on your vision. In my case, discipling men is part of my vision. If that is part of yours, then you are in luck. Samson genuinely helps men grow in Christ.

Is this going to cost my church any money? You'll love this: the answer is no. Samson doesn't cost anything. It doesn't have any money, and it doesn't need any money. In fact, the Samson Society doesn't need much from you. At most, they might ask you for some room to meet in; maybe they'll want to make an announcement. And if you say no, some other pastor will probably say yes.

Will Samson compete with other church programs? Well, for one thing Samson is not a church program. And, yes, it might. Some guys may abandon a program because they want to go to Samson instead. In my opinion, that is not necessarily a bad thing. I'd rather have my guys wholeheartedly involved in Samson than halfheartedly involved in something else. And from my point of view, the Society is a very good thing. Samson is a gift. It will bless the church, and it will advance God's kingdom.

Well, if it's so good, should I make Samson our official men's ministry? I won't tell you what to do, but I am not going to do that. Samson is not really a men's group. It's more a spontaneous fellowship that a pastor can bless without laying hands on it. It is so open-ended that you would probably kill it by making it "official."

Should I personally join Samson? If you are a man, I highly recommend it. I also recommend attending a group that meets in some church other than your own. Why? Two reasons. First, the men in your church are probably in the habit of deferring to your leadership. They'll feel a little inhibited and they won't take full responsibility for this thing if you're in the room. The second reason is even more important. Like me, you need close male friends you can really share with. You need a safe place to speak the truth, no matter what it is, without fear of creating political or personal complications. You and I need to be men before we are pastors. Until Samson, I didn't have much of that. Now I do. And so can any pastor.

The Reverend Thomas McKenzie
Church of the Redeemer,
Nashville, TN

Walking away from a friend is an extraordinary step, one that is seldom necessary in our Society. And while it hasn't happened yet, we can envision a time when it might be necessary to breach the confidentiality of the Society in order to save a third party from serious harm. Obviously, if a guy has confessed plans to kill or rape someone, an intervention is in order. There are other conceivable scenarios under which it might be necessary to break a confidence, but all of them together do not form a foundation wide and stable enough to support the construction of a general policy. Each will need to be judged on its own merits according to the ruling principle of God's people, the Law of Love. And we must always remember that "love covers a multitude of sins" (1 Peter 4:8).

Article Seven

Members are fully authorized to create and distribute, freely or for profit, personal explanations and applications of the Society's principles— if they neither alter nor violate its Charter and do not prohibit others from copying their work.

On August 25, 1991, a twenty-one-year-old Finnish software engineer named Linus Torvalds posted this announcement on an Internet bulletin board:

> I'm doing a (free) operating system (just a hobby, won't be big and professional like gnu) for 386(486) AT clones. This has been brewing since april, and is starting to get ready. I'd like any feedback on things people like/dislike in minix, as my OS resembles it somewhat.[1]

This item caught the attention of a few hackers in the arcane world of computer programming. The young man had an idea for a new operating system for desktop computers, and he was asking for help.

At that time nearly all the world's desktop computers ran on the

Microsoft Windows operating system. The current version, Windows 3.0, sold for $149.95 per copy, enough to make the company's founder the richest man in the world, but it was notoriously buggy. Outside programmers couldn't fix Windows because its source code was a fiercely guarded trade secret. When problems arose, Microsoft customers were forced to rely on the salaried engineers at Microsoft's corporate headquarters in Seattle for patches. Torvalds was proposing something entirely different—a free operating system that anyone could work on. People started sending him suggestions.

A month later, Torvalds posted the first developmental version of his operating system on the Internet: Linux 0.01. Still rather crude, it contained 10,239 lines of code. Torvalds invited other designers to download the system, mess around with it, and send him their improvements.

In October of 1991, Torvalds released the second developmental version—Linux 0.02—and by the end of December he had released nine more versions, each one incorporating improvements made by users. The following month he created a newsgroup archive on the Internet, and his team of volunteer developers began to mushroom. By March of 1992, the network of Linux contributors had succeeded in developing a version capable of running a Windows-style operating system.

Work on the operating system continued at a feverish pace for the next year, and on March 14, 1994, Torvalds released the first distribution version: Linux 1.0.0. It contained 176,250 lines of code. It also contained what became known as the "Linux Kernel," the core section of the code that all the developers agreed not to change.

Torvalds had originally released Linux under a license that forbade any commercial exploitation. Now, however, he took a different tack, releasing it under something known as the General Purpose License (GPL). The GPL gives all Linux users the right to run the software for any purpose, study it, modify it, improve it, and redistribute copies freely or for profit—as long as they do not change the kernel or prohibit others from seeing and using their improvements.

Later on Torvalds would say that issuing Linux under the GPL was "definitely the best thing I ever did."[2]

At about this time, a computer journalist named Eric S. Raymond visited Torvalds to investigate the Linux phenomenon. Raymond was floored by what he found. The project, which now involved thousands of programmers, violated several of Raymond's basic assumptions about the creative process. In a now famous article titled "The Cathedral and the Bazaar," Raymond wrote:

> I believed that the most important software (operating systems and really large tools like Emacs) needed to be built like cathedrals, carefully crafted by individual wizards or small bands of mages working in splendid isolation, with no beta to be released before its time.
>
> Linus Torvalds's style of development—release early and often, delegate everything you can, be open to the point of promiscuity—came as a surprise. No quiet, reverent cathedral-building here—rather, the Linux community seemed to resemble a great babbling bazaar of differing agendas and approaches (aptly symbolized by the Linux archive sites, who'd take submissions from anyone) out of which a coherent and stable system could seemingly emerge only by a succession of miracles.[3]

By the time Linux 2.6.0 (which contained 5,929,913 lines of code) was released in December of 2003, more than a hundred thousand programmers were involved in the project. Corporate giants like IBM and Sun Microsystems were installing the operating system on desktop computers and mainframes, and huge software companies like Oracle and Novell were moving their IT infrastructure to Linux. In Hollywood, major movie studios were so impressed by the system's stability and efficiency that they were producing full-length animated films on Linux machines, and all around the world, governments, businesses, nonprofit organizations, and individuals were using Linux to make the switch from expensive proprietary software to free software.

The development of Linux illustrates the power of collaborative creativity. Wonderful things happen when interested spectators are invited to join an ongoing project as full partners. The kernel of the project must be agreed upon, of course, but when each partner is authorized to address and improve the work of every other partner, the enterprise takes on a life of its own. Problems are spotted. Questions are raised. Ideas are offered. Suggestions are made. Changes are tried. Feedback is given. Lessons are learned, and the project moves forward, gathering speed.

Near the end of "The Cathedral and the Bazaar," Eric S. Raymond made this trenchant observation about what makes a collaborative project viable:

> When you start community-building, what you need to be able to present is a plausible promise. Your program doesn't have to work particularly well. It can be crude, buggy, incomplete, and poorly documented. What it must not fail to do is convince potential co-developers that it can be evolved into something really neat in the foreseeable future.[4]

That's what I hope this book will do. I consider this little volume to be "Samson 1.0.0," the first personal explanation and application of the Society's principles created for general distribution. It is the product of a collaborative effort among people living in Tennessee, California, and Florida—men and women who made invaluable contributions during the Society's initial developmental phase. You'll find many of their names in the Acknowledgments at the end of this book.

And now, on behalf of all my brothers in the Samson Society, I close this book by offering the Society to you.

Would you like to walk with us?

We would enjoy your company, and we could *really* use your help.

Acknowledgments

MANY OF THE MEN AND WOMEN MOST RESPONSIBLE FOR the content of this book must remain anonymous. These broken but extraordinary people, members of various recovery fellowships, have freely shared their lives with me. By word and deed, they have taught me about courage, humility, honesty, faith, and service. God has used them to salvage something worthwhile from my wrecked life, and I am forever in their debt.

This book tells the story of the Samson Society, for which I cannot claim much credit. I was at most a collaborator in the formation of the Society. Scotty Smith and George Grant provided early inspiration and encouragement. Bruce McCurdy and Mike Malloy devoted countless hours to refining the charter, and dozens of other men offered helpful suggestions as it developed. Our local Samson Society was built by the sweat and sacrifice of many men whose wisdom has found its way into the pages of this book. At the risk of overlooking a major contributor, I especially salute Dave Bunker, Glenn McClure, Mark Smeby, Mark Hann, David Hampton, Scott Dente, Joe Shore, Stephen Mason, Dan Haseltine, Jim Colella, Chip Demetri, Jack Wallin, Scott Phillips, John Scudder, Jonathan Kary, Jozef Werner, Christopher Davis, Dave Carlson, Ray Ware, Robert Thompson, Tom Jackson, Rick Pritikin, Will Matheny, John Houmes, Bryan Lautenbach, Marc Kochamba, Art DeArmond,

Michael Creamer, Michael Haggard, Michael Ford, and Charlie Jones for their selfless service to the society and to me. By the time this book is in print, the list of those deserving special mention will probably have doubled.

I am also indebted to the pioneers of other Samson Society meetings, whose experimentation and correspondence have given me glimpses of the forms that Samson can take outside of my own community. In California, Sylvia Lange offered perceptive support from the very beginning. Aaron Porter issued a courageous invitation, and Tom Morris, Dave Mayfield, and John Lohr worked to establish the first Samson fellowships in the Central Coast. (The distinction of the inaugural meeting in the Golden State actually belongs to Tim Morris and his brothers at Simpson University, who met for the first time on January 18, 2006.) Bill Puryear III has carried the torch in the panhandle of Florida, and Frank Moran has left to find Andre in South Africa. Even farther afield, the pioneers of the Samson Sisterhood have carried our message to the opposite sex, adapting the charter and devising a meeting format especially for women. From what Allie tells me, that enterprise is making great progress, thanks to the servant leadership of women I won't even try to name.

Many people sustained me in the writing of this book. My wife, of course, was foremost among them. It was Allie who insisted, at the risk of her own privacy, that I tell the truth or nothing at all, and she graciously endured my frequent physical and mental absences during the yearlong writing project. Many of my brothers in the Samson Society reviewed the manuscript as it developed and offered great feedback. Karen Anderson, who championed the book while it was still an idea, gave invaluable advice. Ray Ware and Don Pape steered it to publishers. David Dunham and Mike Hyatt at Thomas Nelson took the risk of adopting it, and David Moberg and Greg Daniel brought it to their team at W Publishing, who embraced it. I'm especially grateful to my editors, Greg Daniel and Thom Chittom, for their patience with a first-time writer. Their guidance has produced a far better book than I could ever have created on my own.

acknowledgments

Finally, special thanks to Shiloh D'Orazio and all my Coffee Mafia friends at the Five Points Starbucks in Franklin, where this book was written.

Nate Larkin

July 4, 2006

Appendix A

A Suggested Samson Society Meeting Format

Host: My name is _____. Let's open this meeting with prayer, followed by a reading of the Twenty-third Psalm. (*Asks someone to pray, another to read the Twenty-third Psalm.*)

Host: Welcome to this meeting of the Samson Society. We are a company of Christian men.

We are also:

Natural *loners*—who have recognized the dangers of isolation and are determined to escape them

Natural *wanderers*—who are finding spiritual peace and prosperity at home

Natural *liars*—who are now finding freedom in the truth

Natural *judges*—who are learning how to judge ourselves aright

Natural *strongmen*—who are experiencing God's strength as we admit our weaknesses

As Christians, we meet at other times for worship, for teaching, or for corporate prayer. Today, however, we meet to talk. Our purpose is to assist one another in our common journey. We do so by sharing honestly, out of our own personal experience, the challenges and encouragements of daily Christian living in a fallen world.

Our faith rests in the love of God, as it is revealed in his Word and in the life of his Son. This is the Great Fact of the gospel, which is the foundation of our charter. (*Asks someone to read* The Fact.)

Host: Let's take a moment to introduce ourselves. I'll begin and we'll go around the room. Those who wish may give a one-sentence statement of their reason for attending this meeting.

Host: We in the Samson Society have been set upon a Path, a way of living that leads to godliness and freedom. Here is the description of that Path that is given in our charter. (*Asks someone to read* The Path.)

Host: We have now reached the sharing portion of our meeting. In sharing, we speak honestly out of our own experience. We tell the truth about ourselves, knowing that our brothers will listen to us in love and will hold whatever we say in strictest confidence. We try to keep our comments brief, taking care to leave plenty of time for others. We address our statements to the group as a whole rather than directing them toward any one person. As a rule, we refrain from giving advice to others or instructing them during the meeting, believing that such conversations are best reserved for private moments between friends.

The suggested topic today is _____(*choose one of the Suggested Topics for Sharing*)—but we are not confined to that subject. You may speak about any issue that is currently commanding your attention. (*If the group is large, divide into smaller breakout groups for sharing.*) The floor is now open for anyone who wishes to speak.

(*Five minutes before the scheduled end of the meeting, the Host asks whether there are any final thoughts. When all who wish to speak have spoken, the Host says:*)

Host: The formal part of our meeting is now coming to a close, but you are encouraged to stay around afterward to talk, or to adjourn elsewhere for more informal fellowship. Are there any announcements related to this meeting? Any announcements of other Samson Society meetings?

Host: As valuable as they are, these meetings are no substitute for daily Christian friendship. Just as our Lord's first disciples were sent into the world two-by-two, we too should look for at least one Christian companion, a fellow traveler and advisor with whom to share this stretch of the road. We call that person a Silas. (*Choose an experienced member of the group*) _____, would you explain briefly what a Silas is and why we need one? (*Then, at the end of the explanation, say to the whole group*) If you are willing to accept new responsibility as a Silas, please raise your hand.

Before we close, let us reaffirm the Pact under which our Society operates. (*Asks someone to read* The Pact.)

Host: Let's stand and close with prayer. (*Prays simply for the needs expressed, leads in the Lord's Prayer.*)

CHARTER OF
THE SAMSON SOCIETY

THE FACT

1. God exists. In the timeless mystery of the Trinity, He is perfectly harmonious, perfectly whole.

2. God is our Creator. He designed us to live in eternal harmony with Him and each other, and to care for the rest of His creation.

3. Spurning God's fellowship, we all have sinned, forfeiting our created place and losing our spiritual lives.

4. I myself have personally defied God's law and rejected His love. Alienation from Him has produced darkness and chaos in my life, for which I have often blamed others.

5. God has continued to love me, even in my active rebellion, and in Christ has done everything necessary to restore me perfectly to Himself.

6. As I accept responsibility for my sin and find forgiveness in the finished work of Christ, I experience reconciliation with God and am progressively restored to harmony with myself and others.

7. Despite the lingering effects of sin, I am a restored son of the sovereign Lord, whose Spirit is at work in my weakness, displaying His glory and advancing His kingdom.

THE PATH

1. Believing The Fact, I surrender to God in simple faith — making no promises, but merely asking for His aid.

2. I start attending meetings of the Society, and from its members I select a *Silas*, a trustworthy traveling companion for this stretch of the road.

3. In honest detail, I describe to God and to my Silas the course and consequences of my attempts to live apart from God.

4. Encouraged by my Silas and others, I develop the daily disciplines of prayer, study and self-examination. I abandon self-help, asking God instead to do for me what I cannot do for myself.

5. I choose to trust the Body of Christ, weighing the wisdom of my friends when facing decisions and seeking their strength when confronted by temptation.

6. When I can do so without injuring anyone, I make amends for damage I have caused. If direct amends are impossible or inadvisable, I demonstrate my repentance in other ways.

7. I offer myself as a Silas to others. Each day I ask God for the grace to seek His kingdom rather than my own, to serve those He places in my path rather than serving myself.

THE PACT

1. God is the sole owner of the Samson Society and its only authority. No member may speak for the entire Society.

2. All members of the Society are equals — friends and fellow servants, bound by love and honor. No member may command the obedience of another.

3. The Society owns no property, collects no dues or fees, pays no salaries, incurs no debts.

4. The Society is an extension of the Church Universal. It is not a corporate entity and can make no contracts with congregations, denominations, causes or campaigns, regardless of their merit.

5. Any two or more persons who believe the Fact, who agree to follow this Path and join this Pact, may initiate a meeting of the Samson Society.

6. We hold in strictest confidence any personal information shared by other members, unless permission to divulge it is given by any whom its disclosure might affect.

7. Members are fully authorized to create and distribute, freely or for profit, personal explanations and applications of the Society's principles — if they neither alter nor violate its Charter and do not prohibit others from copying their work.

Appendix B

Suggested Topics for Sharing

Acceptance	Compromise	Enemies	Gambling
Accomplishment	Confidentiality	Enlightenment	Generosity
Adulthood	Confrontation	Envy	Gentleness
Adventure	Confusion	Escape	Goals
Advice	Contentment	Excitement	Goodness
Anger	Control	Exercise	Gratitude
Argument	Counsel	Expectations	Greed
Awe	Courage	Failure	Grief
Beauty	Covetousness	Fairy tales	Growth
Begging	Creativity	Faith	Gullibility
Belief	Criticism	Faithfulness	Happiness
Betrayal	Deceit	Family	Hatred
Blame	Defeat	Fantasy	Health
Blindness	Defensiveness	Father	Heroes
Boredom	Denial	Fatigue	Hoarding
Bravery	Destructiveness	Fear	Holiness
Busyness	Determination	Fighting	Honesty
Certainty	Diet	Focus	Hope
Chaos	Disappointment	Foolishness	Humility
Clarity	Disclosure	Forgetfulness	Hunger
Communication	Dishonesty	Forgiveness	Identity
Comparison	Distraction	Freedom	Indulgence
Compassion	Education	Friendship	Injuries
Competition	Encouragement	Fulfillment	Insanity

Integrity	Nature	Respect	Surrender
Intimacy	Neediness	Rest	Suspicion
Intoxication	Normality	Responsibility	Teamwork
Intrigue	Nourishment	Revelation	Temptation
Inventory	Obedience	Righteousness	Tenderness
Isolation	Patience	Risk	Tolerance
Joy	Peace	Romance	Toughness
Kindness	Perfection	Sabotage	Transparency
Knowledge	Persistence	Sacrifice	Trust
Laughter	Politeness	Sadness	Truth
Learning	Power	Sanity	Unbelief
Liberty	Powerlessness	Secrets	Understanding
Listening	Productivity	Self-Care	Vagueness
Longing	Profit	Self-Centeredness	Value
Loss	Promises	Self-Discipline	Victory
Love	Prayer	Selfishness	War
Lust	Pride	Service	Waste
Lying	Progress	Sex	Weakness
Martyrdom	Quietness	Shame	Willingness
Masculinity	Quitting	Sleep	Wisdom
Medication	Rage	Solitude	Women
Meditation	Reconciliation	Spirit	Wonder
Memory	Recreation	Stealing	Work
Mission	Regret	Strength	Worry
Mistakes	Relapse	Stewardship	Worship
Moderation	Relaxation	Study	Wounds
Mother	Resentment	Superstition	Youth

☠ Notes ☠

Chapter 12

1. Posted by Linus Torvalds on http://www.radiotux.de 25 August 1991.
2. Interview found on http://kde.sw.com.sg/food/linus.html with Linus Torvalds, 11 November 1997.
3. Eric Raymond, *Cathedral and the Bazaar: Musings on Linux and Open Source by an Accidental Revolutionary* (Sebastopol, CA: O'Reilly Media, 2001). Article can also be found at http://catb.org/~esr/writings/cathedral-bazaar/.
4. Ibid.

All the men and women involved in this book have given me full permission to tell their stories and to use their real names. Some also requested that I change names and recognizable details, usually to protect the privacy of children and other family members. I have honored their requests. For the same reasons, I also changed a few details about my own story. The essentials of every story, however, are entirely true and were told to me by those involved.